Pyongyang Lessons

North Korea From Inside the Classroom

Stewart Lone

About the Book

From 2010-12, the author went every six months to teach at two major secondary schools in Pyongyang, the capital of North Korea. Over these visits, he spent hundreds of hours teaching several hundred teenage schoolboys, and some schoolgirls, in the classroom and in informal conversation groups. In this book, he recounts his experiences and presents what he learned about their lives, study, ideas, interests, and ambitions.

Who, for example, would have thought, in a society routinely dismissed as reclusive and repressive, that schoolchildren learn about Ireland, about Maoris and their customs, have discussions on being creative and on animal rights, that young boys idolise a Barcelona footballer, and that a favourite joke concerns a North Korean army deserter?

What emerged through these experiences and observations, in school and in candid talks with teachers, officials, and a wide variety of ordinary people, is an intimate portrait, nowhere else available, of the human face of Pyongyang and of a generation set one day to lead the country.

Stewart Lone is professor of Asian social history at the University of New South Wales, Australia.

Pyongyang Lessons: North Korea From Inside the Classroom

© Stewart Lone 2013

Published by Create Space, an Amazon company

isbn13- 978-1482729757

isbn10-148272975x

'It is not what we endure that matters; what matters is how we endure it'

Seneca

Above all, this is for Yimei, my extraordinary wife who endured decades of hardship in China with a song in her heart

Foreword

What follows is an account of what I experienced and observed over the course of several working visits between 2010-2012 to two highly respected middle schools in Pyongyang, the capital of North Korea. I present this account without any intended bias; not once, in all the hundreds of hours of my teaching and conversation with colleagues and students, did anyone in Pyongyang ever attempt to limit or regulate what I said or heard. I repay that trust here by being equally open and honest. The book is offered to those who wish to understand the human face of North Korea; those wanting only horror stories and the world-as-freakshow may look elsewhere. To those who might insist that what I saw or heard was only the capital and not the 'real' Korea, my answer is simple; when you see it, then you tell me about it. At more than ten percent of the population of the DPRK, Pyongyang is real, whatever you may think. It also is changing, and rapidly at that. In that sense, this is only a snapshot of one moment in time.

This book is completed with the help and encouragement of many people in various countries. Rather than name them individually (they know who they are), I shall thank them collectively. The book itself is dedicated to my wife, Yimei, but also to my students, both in Pyongyang and at the University of NSW campus in Canberra. You are the reason I am here.

Starting at One End

It is mid-December 2011, late on a Saturday afternoon in Beijing. Did I really leave Pyongyang only this morning? Now I am weaving through the anarchic, murderously carefree traffic, heading into the James Joyce Bar to address the Foreign Correspondents Club of China. My good friend, Kōichi, who is the Beijing correspondent for one of the major Japanese newspapers, has arranged for me to give a talk about my latest working visit as a school teacher in Pyongyang. There is a problem, however; after just two hours in Beijing, my throat is swelling and my head is aching from the poison which masquerades in this city as air (one of the most common, and reasonable, boasts in Pyongyang is that the air is largely unpolluted). Kōichi has told me in the taxi coming here that there is an on-going dispute in Beijing (I also see this reported on Japanese TV a few days later); the US embassy issues a daily assessment of the capital's air quality, generally ranging from 'dangerous' to 'run for the hills!'. The Beijing authorities, however, issue their own assessment which flits between 'no worries' to 'not terribly good' (I am stamping my own terms on reality here but the point remains true). It seems many Beijingers believe the US and the grit in their own eyes and throats rather than the complacency of the local government. Could this be the start of another upswell of popular outrage, another 1989? Before I can be distracted by this dramatic possibility, I enter the bar and see that there is a roaring log fire beside the place where I am to speak: poisoned and now dehydrated! No, the conditions are not ideal. However, I see there are about forty seats arranged for the audience, and there are plenty of people milling around the bar with just minutes before I'm due to start. It is time to work but what to say? I have not had a moment even to gather my thoughts after all the activity of the past few weeks. Even late last night in Pyongyang, I was busy proof-reading a new draft textbook for one of the teachers (all the while hoping that the electricity in the hotel would not cut out and I could keep my promise to finish it before my departure). Now, here I am. Again, what to say? I can keep it simple; always a good idea when you know nothing of your audience. The advertisement told them I would be speaking about the schoolchildren of two academically elite schools in Pyongyang, their activities, their interests, and their ambitions. So be it. I will structure the talk as clearly as possible: explain how I came to be at the school, tell the audience what the children learn, how they learn, what they enjoy, and what they want to be. Of course, that is not the whole story of the past few weeks. Not by a long way...

Day 1.

Beijing airport in late November: I am waiting for the coach which takes us across the tarmac to the Air Koryo 'plane. It is the usual mix of passengers: North Korean citizens loaded up with purchases of everything from tiny computers to large TVs, bands of Chinese holidaymakers, and one or two groups of European tourists all nervously excited by the prospect of visiting what is usually presented to them as the most bizarre and repressive society on earth. If they came as voyeurs, I think they may be disappointed by its normality. Indeed, one of the major aims of this book is to show just how 'normal' are the daily lives of ordinary people, at work, rest, play, and in their likes, loves, laughter, ambitions and fears.

Despite the racy corporate video before take-off, all surging jets and dynamic human activity, the Air Koryo fleet is composed of Soviet-era craft, presumably from the 1970s. It doesn't bother me. Some of the fittings don't fit and some of the seats are not entirely stable but the 'plane goes up and when it comes down, we are always at our destination. That is all that matters. I do have one criticism, however. Every time I take this flight, one of the stewardesses always seems to spray me with one of the drinks. Am I being singled out for this treatment or is it just part of the unique Air Koryo service? The previous time was in May and the heat inside the 'plane was so intense that the European passengers repeatedly asked the cabin staff to turn on the fans. Nothing happened (maybe there were no fans) so, on that occasion, I was quite content to be sprayed by water, tea or anything cool. But when it happens this time, I am less forgiving and I look at the young sky waitress coldly. The other one pulling the drinks cart, slightly older and clearly more experienced, apologises quickly in English but the culprit just stands, frozen with fear at my unforgiving face. Immediately, I feel sorry for my reaction and, when she returns with the cart later, I ask her very gently for some water (in a cup) and make sure that I thank her politely. My reward is a timid smile.

At the airport, the immigration officer is, for the first time in my experience, a woman, her hat set high atop the raised hairstyle favoured by women in official posts (it is a style which reminds me of the well-to-do in Edwardian England). She takes my passport, studies it, then, to my surprise, asks me; 'You live in Australia?' This is the first time anyone on the desk has ever spoken to me. Is it a sign of welcome, I wonder, a kind of 'So, here you are again...' I smile and agree that, yes, I do live in Australia, but I resist the urge to extend the conversation and complicate matters by adding that I am not, in fact, an Australian citizen (hence my European passport). Next is the baggage check. On my last visit, the officer had looked at all the textbooks, DVDs, and laptops I had brought as gifts for various schools, but not unkindly. I had explained these were presents and that my colleagues from the Pyongyang schools were doubtless already waiting in the airport and could vouch for me. Having enough Korean language to convey these things obviously made the whole encounter much easier and more pleasant. Today, the officials barely check my bag; they ask me if I have a computer, I show it to them, and they wave me on my way. I am beginning to feel genuinely at 'home'. Then, as one of them hands me back my passport, I already see my two *compadres*, Manager Kim and Teacher Kim, emerging from the waiting crowd.

Teacher Kim is the elder statesman of the English-language teachers at the two schools where I work. He helped to train some of the younger staff. He is in his early forties, of medium height, with a relatively long, thin face which, while handsome, does give him on occasion the look of someone who worries too much (he also smokes too much, something about which we are in constant dispute). He is soft-voiced, quick to laugh, endlessly, endlessly patient, and an easy man to be with. Manager Kim deals with student recruitment and resources for the two schools. He also is of medium height but with a barrel chest which makes him seem far taller than he is. This is aided by his enormous personality; this is a man who just loves life! He and I often joke together, sometimes fight together, but always work together. With him, I am never in doubt that we are jointly engaged in something substantial, challenging, difficult, but also hugely rewarding.

After the usual hugs and kind words, we are in the car heading for the hotel. Sometimes Manager Kim arranges a luxury vehicle, typically a Mercedes or BMW (there are enough of both on the streets of Pyongyang to make any resident of Stuttgart or Munich feel proud). Sometimes, it is an aging, wheezing mini-bus. Today I get the BMW (tomorrow, as I discover, I get the mini-bus). In the car, Manager Kim brings me up to date on certain things. There are, it seems, two major problems these days for the people of Korea. One is that the supply of coal is erratic: Korea has undeveloped mineral wealth but it may be that its coal supplies are in decline and this, just as the winter is approaching, means frequent power cuts. Well, this has happened so often in the past, everyone just adapts; when the power goes out, you wait or, if it's night and you have a pocket torch, as so many people do, then you switch it on and carry on (cooking seems to be done mainly by gas so meals are not a major hurdle). The other problem is that the weather thus far has been so mild for so long that the basic food of Koreans, kimchi, which needs the cold to ferment, has not matured as it should. It sounds slightly trivial but food obviously is fundamental to one's enjoyment of life, whatever political system you favour. Indeed, the traditional Korean definition of paradise really boils down to having a roof over your head and a bowl of rice with kimchi in your hand. Sour kimchi suggests I will be meeting some unhappy colleagues and contacts in the coming days.

We arrive at my usual hotel in west Pyongyang. This is Chongnyon or Youth Hotel. It is a vast, 30-storey rectangular slab of dark concrete and glass, as anonymous as a giant's tombstone. Having said that, how many hotels built in the past forty years have anything to distinguish them from the outside except their corporate logo (a Marriott is a Sheraton is a Holiday Inn...) In my experience, this is especially the case in Japan where even the room looks the same in every hotel and sometimes one only knows where one is by looking at the corporate stationery. So, Chongnyon Hotel is no better or worse than any other hotel picked at random in any other country. With one exception: its cavernous marble lobby in winter, even a mild winter, is, by common consent among we three, the coldest place in Korea. There are three doormen at the entrance, two young and one middle-aged. They always give me a salute and a smile as I pass but how they survive these months in just a greatcoat and gloves, I cannot say. Doors in Pyongyang buildings usually do not open directly; there are often two layers of doorway and some twist or turn one has to make to go through the second, or one goes through a revolving door, all in an attempt to slow the influx of freezing air (sometimes, as at one of the schools where I work, a heavy canvas curtain is hung between the inner and outer doors). Even so, my heart goes out to these doormen every time I see them. In winter, the reception staff wear thick padded jackets and one rarely sees their hands (except when they are dealing with calls). The girls in the lobby coffee shop also wear light-coloured, thickly-layered winter parkas and, as I later learn, frequently retreat behind a closed screen where there is a cot and a very good heater. After signing in at the front desk, we three sit down in the coffee shop for a while and plan out the next few weeks. The chill quickly starts to creep into our bones and the planning becomes more hurried and less rigorous.

Back to the Beginning

My first serious encounter with Korea was as a graduate student in Japan in the mid-1980s. This was not North Korea, however, but the South. In Kyoto where I lived and studied modern Japanese history, there was a sizable Korean community. One of my graduate colleagues engaged with Korean history introduced me to an amazing personality. He was a renaissance man; literary scholar, businessman, gourmet, and political activist. His political activities were focused around a seemingly lifelong campaign to have his elder brothers released from a South Korean prison. By that point, the brothers had already spent years in prison for their part in protests against the military dictators who dominated South Korea from the early 1960s to the late 1980s. That was my first impression of Korea: militarism and repression but in the South.

As for North Korea, I had no reason or special desire at that time to question the news reports which ran exactly the same line, year after year, and continue largely to do so into the 21st century; that is, a regime mad, bad, and dangerous. In time, however, I did grow weary of seeing exactly the same footage on every TV news report about the North; it was of a scientist (or at least a man in a white coat) walking around what was assumed to be the control room of some terrifying weapons program (but could just as easily have been a clip from any space age movie about 'dangerous Orientals' and their devilish schemes).

A turning point was around 1994. On Channel 4 in England, there was a travel documentary in which a serious, respected and very down-to-earth British music journalist, Andy Kershaw, visited Pyongyang. What struck me was the general ease of his interactions with the people he met, from officials to soldiers to housewives. It was the first time I had ever seen anyone present the North Korean people as *people* instead of as nameless, faceless automatons of a despotic regime. It was a breath of fresh air.

The decisive moment came in 2006. By that time, I had been teaching Asian history for some years at the University of New South Wales campus inside the Australian Defence Force Academy. One of my upper-level students wanted to do a research project on contemporary China and North Korea. It seemed a challenge to both of us and, precisely for that reason, we both embraced the idea. Early in the project, I suggested to her that she try and visit Pyongyang as part of her research. She was surprised, assuming from all the media demonization of the North that no outsider, at least from the West, would be allowed entry. There was, at that time, a North Korean embassy in the Australian capital; a simple 'phone call and we discovered that a local travel company in Sydney had the contract from Pyongyang to send over regular tourist groups or individuals. There seemed to be no problem and she was thrilled at the prospect of seeing for herself a place which had only ever been presented to her as a nightmare land. In practice, however, it was the Australian army which was the obstacle; young officers and officer cadets are forbidden on grounds of their own security from visiting many countries around the world, including Israel, large parts of India, and also North Korea. To assuage her disappointment, and also to nourish my own curiosity, I then offered to make a trip in her stead and report back on what I saw. Thus, in the spring of 2006, I made my first visit to the North.

What I saw, and more importantly what I heard, on that first trip convinced me that I had been deliberately misled for years about North Korean society. Instead of secretiveness and coldness, I was treated with kindness and openness by many of the people I met. In particular, my two constant tour guides were endlessly helpful but also, to my surprise, great fun (when I pointed out that an army jeep we saw in east Korea had seat-covers carrying the Playboy Bunny logo, they thought it was wickedly funny). They told me many things, often with complete frankness, and also told me some fine stories (plus one or two quite risqué jokes). The one that remains clearest in my memory dates from our day-trip to Panmunjom, the stand-off and stare-off site between the North and South militaries. I was given a tour by a North Korean army officer who was courtesy personified. At the end of the tour, I had thanked him warmly. One of my guides, as we headed back to our minibus, had then spoken of an earlier Swedish tourist who had tried to make a fool of that same officer. At the conclusion of his tour, the Swede had offered him a cigarette. As the officer took it, however, the Swede had challenged him, saying, "That's an American cigarette – how can you smoke an American cigarette?!" The officer then withdrew the cigarette, looked at it calmly for a moment, and then replied: "To you, I am smoking it. To me, I am burning it." That, I thought, was game, set and match to the officer.

There were many other examples, of course, where I met the pleasantly unexpected. At the Pyongyang Central Gallery in the heart of the city, one of the middle-aged female guides spent close to an entire afternoon, at my request, showing and explaining in detail to me much of the magnificent collection of works ancient to modern. At my hotel, two of the young women in the lobby shop were cheerful and cheeky. When I said to them, I wanted to buy something to snack on in the evening, they giggled and directed me to a shelf full of boxed roots. As I examined the box closer, they stood close, still giggling. As it dawned on me this was nature's version of Viagra, the two exploded with laughter. Not quite what I had in mind, I explained, and they laughed even harder. As I bought some biscuits instead, they told me they didn't have the right change in euros (although the euro is the official foreign currency in the North, I only ever saw Koreans carrying US dollars). So, despite the regulation which bars foreigners from receiving North Korean *won*, they just gave me a few local notes along with an amused finger to the lips of "sshhh, tell no one!"

With all of this, I immediately resolved at the end of my first visit to return, for a longer time and in a deeper form, and to find out more about this fascinating place. So, upon my return to Australia, I revisited the Korean embassy and offered my services as a teacher, as and when required. In 2010, the Korea-Australia Friendship Society in Pyongyang received a dynamic new head of operations and I, in turn, received an invitation to work at two schools, helping the pupils better to use and understand the English language. The invitation was not exactly for the faint of heart. There would be upwards of twenty-five hours per week of classroom teaching, plus another ten hours of informal lessons, as well meetings with teachers and consultation over the textbook and materials presently in use. I would be required to pay all my own expenses of travel, to and from Pyongyang, plus the use of a hire car and driver while working, as well as of food and accommodation. Who could resist?

First Sunday

It is 9am on a winter's Sunday and, having arrived in Pyongyang only the day before, I am now standing in the park and woodland grounds of Mangyongdae. This is on the western outskirts of Pyongyang, actually not very far from the school where I am teaching this time around. We are visiting the tiny farmhouse which is the family home of the DPRK's founding father (I use this term, paternal not divine, very deliberately), Kim Ilsung. I have been here at least three times before and, on the past two occasions, I have been paired with the same guide, a friendly, lively young woman in her mid or late twenties, dressed (in winter) in a long black coat with a fur collar; bare protection against the cold, I think. She is notable among the exclusively female guides at this, arguably the most emotive and important site in the country, because she speaks English with a rich, warm Russian burr. I am happy to see her again but, today, it is truly freezing and I have no feeling below the knees. I am accompanied by a group of about ten of the schoolboys whom I taught on my last visit in May. Even though their jackets look thin, they are clearly warmer than me; I envy them their youth and, on the pretext of hearing the guide more clearly, I encourage them to gather closer to her and me, thus using them as a human windbreak (it occurs to me in retrospect, with their black jackets and fresh, smooth-skinned faces, we probably look from the outside like a sheltering herd of penguins).

The first time I met the guide, she was reciting the story of the Kim family's poverty and the young Kim's revolutionary determination exactly as it is scripted (I had heard precisely the same recitation from another guide on my initial visit). There was nothing unusual about this; at tourist spots in other countries, I had heard the same stories in the same language and tones from different guides over the years. The main theme of the story at Mangyongdae is the importance of enduring hardship – especially domination by others - through an unshakable belief in ultimate success: it is the key narrative in North Korean history and is illustrated by one of the family's utensils. This is a misshapen water or cereals jar, twisted as if it were crippled, bought a century ago by Kim's grandmother despite the ridicule of all the other villagers. One day, she is said to have declared, we will overcome this poverty but such things as this jar will remind us of what we once were forced to suffer. On that particular day, however, I had stopped listening to the guide's story and instead was listening more to her use and pronunciation of English. Noticing this, she interrupted her recitation and asked me, rather worriedly: 'Is there something wrong? Is my English not good?' This was when she explained, even confessed, to me that she was fully trained in Russian but, as there were now far fewer Russian-speaking tourists than those who understood something of English, she had been forced to reinvent herself and, behind the script, she really was painfully anxious about her ability as an English guide. I felt sorry for her and helped her as best I could by praising her when she was right, and nudging her when she was wrong. I found that nearly all of the guides I met at major historical sites and museums across Pyongyang wanted to be reassured that their English was intelligible at least and, for preference, as close to perfect as it could be. Each time, they were ready to set aside their confident front in order to ask me about a word or phrase, and whether there was not a better, more compelling way to say the same thing; it was always something I welcomed because it allowed us to talk to each other instead of me being relegated simply to the position of mute audience as they went through their paces. Since that first meeting, the guide at Mangyongdae and I had become friends and she always greeted me warmly. Today, I need all the warmth I can get (on the pretext of leaving me alone with my ladyfriend, and my pupils, Manager Kim very sensibly is taking shelter somewhere).

Rest Day

On my first Sunday afternoon, Manager Kim, Teacher Kim and I, fortified and warmed by lunch at one of Pyongyang's busy restaurants (not, I am glad to say, one of the Chinese-operated McDonalds clones), returned to the hotel and were again discussing the coming week's schedule in the Chongnyon coffee shop. Located as it was to one side of the huge marble foyer, it was perpetually cold but it was, albeit briefly, convenient as a place to chat and, as long as you left before frostbite set in, it was also nice to be in the company of the three waitresses, all of whom were pretty, pleasant (and chatty) young women in their mid-twenties.

Ms. Pak at the Chongnyon Hotel coffee shop

Generally, Manager Kim would have a glass of beer (always commenting on its quality, whether good or bad) and Teacher Kim would have a beer and a cigarette. Seeing this, Manager Kim would always say, 'Cigarettes. Yes, I have given them up. My wife is very happy.' Then he would pick up the packet on the table and add, 'I will try just one; to remind myself why I have given up.' He would then take one of Teacher Kim's cigarettes, light it, inhale a few times, and then, with a look of distaste, stub it out. I saw this performance at least several times in the weeks I was there.

As this was the day before the start of teaching, Manager Kim wanted to make absolutely sure that I agreed with his schedule. The classroom teaching was fixed but the extra-curricular activities were open. On my first teaching trip, he and I had had a stand-up row late in the visit about how he kept changing this part of the schedule every day without informing me. As a result, on the second visit, he had done as I originally asked and arranged nothing but teaching. On this longer third visit, he had suggested just one trip to a museum or site of interest in the city each week. We talked over the possibilities (for some reason, he seemed especially keen to include an ostrich farm in our itinerary but, having no interest in ostriches myself, I found ways to circumvent this). The idea was to take a small group of pupils on each occasion and have them explain to me in English what they saw or what they heard from the guides. It all looked good.

After we finished our discussion, Manager Kim went off to work his mobile 'phone for the rest of the afternoon while Teacher Kim and I remained at the coffee shop. At that moment, the cafe 'phone rang and the most self-assured and most sociable of the waitresses, the elegant Ms. Pak (a graduate of Teacher Kim's school), answered. I saw her looking in my direction. When she put the 'phone down, she spoke to Teacher Kim who then translated for me (she could have told me in English and, on later evenings, we were to spend up to an hour in broken conversation). The call was from Huiran, the hotel masseuse whom I had visited almost daily on my previous stays as she regularly unlocked my back muscles and prepared me for the next day's teaching. She had, I was told, a question for me; what time that afternoon was I coming for treatment? I was intrigued; how did she know I was here, either at the hotel generally or at the cafe at that moment? Of course, the answer was obvious, as she told me a few minutes later when I re-entered her two-room studio on the second floor. No hint of microphones or CCTV (I rarely saw any CCTV camera in the whole of Pyongyang, unlike the five million plus staring you in the face across every town and city in Britain); she had simply seen me as she crossed the lobby.

Huiran was one of the reasons I felt so comfortable at the Chongnyon Hotel. Like some others in the hotel, she had been generous and patient from the very first moment we met. As with Ms. Pak, she had a few words of English and I had a few words of Korean so we managed to get by. If I did not understand something she said, she would repeat it and, if I still did not understand, she would simply ask 'mullayo?' – 'you don't understand?' and let it be but also be neither discouraged nor impatient. She was a tiny woman, five feet or less, in her mid-thirties but with a huge smile and an infectious laugh. I thought of her as the most benevolent of pixies. From the first few days, however, we had a running joke. She would press here and there on my back and ask me, 'Appayo?' – 'does it hurt?' – and, if I said 'Yes!', instead of just 'yes', she would laugh, especially when she pressed on my back and heard the 'kik kik kik' of ribs going back into place. I assume the laugh was apologetic but I took to telling her that my pain was obviously her pleasure, and that she must be exceptionally happy on those days when I came to her in exceptional pain. She agreed, not seriously, merely joining in the joke. Later in this visit, however, I strained both hamstrings playing soccer with the schoolboys and then strained them again a few days later doing the same thing. When I told her mischievously that I had promised to play a third game the following day and would probably end up in hospital, she was genuinely distressed and asked me to take care that such a thing never happened. Before moving to the hotel, she had worked as a therapist for some years in a Pyongyang hospital and clearly had seen too much pain and probably not a few patients who did not live to go home. I ended the joke right then and there but when I did return the following day, muscles duly stretched and torn yet further, she did seem to take unusual delight in pressing here and there and asking 'appayo?'

On the subject of pain, there were two beds in Huiran's studio, separated by a large wooden screen. Her friend and co-worker used the other when there were two customers. She was an energetic, perhaps slightly younger woman, much taller and broader but perpetually suffering from some cold or other (Huiran told me in Korean that her friend had a particular ailment which I could not initially recognise until I realised that Koreans had borrowed the English term – it was 'acute bronchitis'). Only one time did I receive treatment while there was another customer in the room. His head protruded just beyond the wooden screen and I could see he was probably in his late twenties or early thirties. What struck me, however, was that he kept saying 'Appa! Uh, appa!'- 'Ow! Ow!'. Huiran's colleague had worked on me once and I knew her to be a fine masseuse so I was certain she was not the cause of his pain. Either the young fellow had major health problems, and probably was not long for this world, or he was one of the most fragile and timid characters in the country. How he had endured his mandatory three years military service was a question I could not even begin to answer.

Back to School

It is Monday, 8.20am. Manager Kim, Teacher Kim and I are waiting on the steps of Chongnyon Hotel. We are late; very late. We have been waiting for about 10 minutes but still our vehicle (the aging mini-bus, not the shiny BMW) is nowhere in sight. Manager Kim has been on the mobile 'phone twice already. The driver is on his way, we are told, but the traffic is heavy. I am not pleased at this start. I am here to work, not to wait for a bus. We all pace up and down the entrance of the hotel, partly out of frustration and partly to keep warm. Finally, the vehicle arrives, we jump in, and then head off the short distance to the school (I suggest to Teacher Kim it would only take forty minutes to walk and would be good, brisk exercise – he smiles and says nothing). I am now hoping that we will not encounter one of the more intrusive traffic policewomen. They are all tall, long-legged, stern-faced and the body language suggests they are as tough as nails; when they whistle, you stop, and the cold intensity of their glare makes the stereotype New York traffic cop look as cuddly and harmless as Elmer Fudd. There is a popular film from some years back which presents the traffic policewomen as warm, gentle, maternal people but I suspect the real policewomen dismiss this as candy for the masses (the film is interesting, however, for its depiction of truck and van-drivers as serial rule-breakers). Fortunately, they are looking elsewhere this morning so we quickly (but not too quickly) exit the main roads, just beyond the vast new museum of Taekwondo, turn into a residential area of broad apartment blocks and some houses, and head towards the school. As we approach, I notice that all the trees have been cleared from in front of the school, or College to use its official title, so that the entirety of its panorama can now be seen from the road.

22

조선예술영화

네거리초병

Korean Film

A Traffic Controller
on Crossroads

NTSC   COLOR – 59 MINS

Smiles and flowers? A popular film presenting the more gentle face of the traffic

policewomen.

I had hardly realised before just how large it is, this school first built in the mid-1960s with just a handful of staff and children and now with a total of 2,000 pupils and over 400 teachers. On the main steps, the slight figure of the now-aging principal, Professor Oh, is waiting with Mr. Bak, the English department head, and the latter's assistant and my delightful friend, Mrs. Kim. The professor has already been told why we are late so we keep the welcomes and the explanations brief as classes start at 8.30am. The professor is of a very like mind to me in many things and he shoos me off to class (but not before a quick handshake with the always amiable, if bear-like, Mr. Bak and, with Mrs. Kim, tall, slim, high-cheekboned and ever smiling, a longer hug).

It takes some nerve to walk into a classroom and take charge of a group of young people. Anyone who does not feel a moment of self-doubt is lacking in self-awareness – Socrates insisted that the limits of his knowledge were so vast that he could not in all conscience call himself a teacher. True enough for him and even more so for the rest of us, but when you are the only non-Korean these pupils aged 14 may ever encounter in their school careers (Tim Kearns, from New Zealand, was a pioneer teacher here but that was before these boys' time), then you have an enormous responsibility but also you have to set aside any doubt and convince yourself that you genuinely have something to offer them. That is what I told myself every single time I opened a classroom door in Pyongyang.

I have a routine whenever I enter a class in Korea. I stride in looking at the window opposite the door, place my bag on the teacher's desk, turn to face the class, and smile. Then I pause for a moment and, in silence, survey the group. In Korea, the class stands whenever the teacher enters or leaves the room; pupils also stand when they address the teacher and wait until instructed to sit down again. When offering something to the teacher, such as a piece of their homework, they use both hands as a mark of courtesy. So here we are again: twenty boys to a class, all standing, all smiling back at me. After a count of three, I start with the expected greeting and question: 'Good morning boys. How are you?' As one voice, they usually shout back: 'We are fine! How are you?' Depending on the decibel level, which can be rock concert deafening, I either continue or I repeat the question in a whisper and get a much softer reply. Later in the visit, I tell the boys that it is unnatural and even dull to give the same answer every day (even though they insist to me on their honour that they really are fine) and that, just occasionally, they should tell me that they are 'not too bad', 'can't complain', 'got a touch of cold' or something similar (there is a bias at both schools towards British English so phrases like these are not entirely unwelcome). By the end of my trip, I am getting a babble of different and discordant replies to this innocuous question. I actually feel rather guilty about introducing this kind of 'honesty'.

After the initial greeting, I explain each day what I propose to do during the lesson. Normally, I aim for three activities each class in order to keep it interesting and varied (school runs from Monday through Saturday so variety is essential to keep up the energy levels, not least those of the teacher). I follow this pattern over the following weeks: first, introduce some idioms or words which may spark their interest, especially if they relate to computer studies which, along with mathematics and English, is one of their most important subjects; second, choose something from their textbook so that they can be on familiar territory for a while; third, introduce something where they can be more active, more creative, such as a story from their experience or imagination. Today, having outlined the plan, we are off and running and will barely pause for breath over the next three weeks.

In the Classroom

The rooms I use in both schools are light and airy. This is in contrast to some of the rooms at my home campus in Australia which have neither natural air nor light but do have drowsy and disinterested students. In Pyongyang, the space comfortably accommodates the number of pupils in each class; twenty at one school, twenty-five at the other in the city centre. There is no sense of a crush and the teacher can quite easily navigate around the desks, with the exception only of those at the centre of a row of three. In my experience, the room belongs to the pupils; the boys, or girls, stay put and the teachers for different subjects come to them. Obviously this is different for science subjects needing a laboratory. Within the room, each student has his or her own desk but, much as at my own school when I was their age, some of them exchange places every month or so to get a different view of things or because of changing friendships. On each desk, there is a computer; within the schools, Dell is the maker of choice but, at the elite Kim Ilsung University, the latest computers are HP (some school officials I met favoured Toshiba). There is a TV monitor at the front of the class for displaying visual materials. There is also often a vase of flowers either at the front or back. These (artificial in winter) are probably bought from the many street flower stalls which exist all over the city but flourish especially near big institutions like a school (flowers are a very popular choice of gift for special occasions and celebrations).

Other decoration normally consists of a national map, and two portrait photos of Kim Ilsung and Kim Jong'il. The photos are usually above the blackboard (or whiteboard). The thing that I noticed about these, however, was that they were so very different from all the other public images of the two leaders, especially the one on the Kim Ilsung badge which most, but not all, adults wore daily. Instead, the classroom photos showed the two men in youth, dressed in what appeared to be a school uniform, without glasses and, surprisingly, without smiles. The point seemed to be that the schoolchildren were being taught to think of the leaders as just like themselves; young, studious, and serious. Yet, every other picture of the Kims, on posters, hoardings, calendars etc. invariably showed them beaming with pleasure, bespectacled, in older age; a cheerful, amiable father or grandfather.

Even in winter, the classrooms did not feel cold. At least, I did not feel it but then, during this trip from November to December, I did come down with three separate colds in three weeks (too much chatting in the evenings with Ms. Pak in the freezing café!). I should add that I frequently taught from deep inside a thick coat made in Germany and with the kind of thermal technology that would make NASA proud; to this, I added an inner coat and scarf. When I asked about the pupils, one of my colleagues told me with great surety, 'young boys don't feel the cold!' It is true that I rarely saw any boy absent from sickness and I never saw anyone shivering in class. Certainly, I could see no evidence of a heater, even when the temperature outside was about minus nine degrees. I did see one concession to comfort, however. When I instructed the boys to work as a group in class, one of them rose from his desk to reveal he had changed from his outdoor shoes into a luxurious pair of big, fluffy slippers (had he been my size, I might have been tempted to swap).

One of the fixed ideas overseas about younger Koreans in the North is that the famine years of 1994-2000 have led to a general stunting of their physical growth. There are even some foreign observers who insist that famine still occurs in the North and so one might expect in the coming years several generations of undersized adults. I can only comment on what I have seen. To date, I have taught over four hundred teenage boys in two Pyongyang schools; their family backgrounds and place of origin are diverse. Naturally, the majority of them come from the Pyongyang region. However, there are plenty who come from the northernmost parts of the country, and others from everywhere in-between. Moreover, the height range of these pupils is equally diverse. Among the fourteen-year olds, there are those who are as tall as, or taller than, their adult male teachers, and there are those over whom I (only the same height as Dustin Hoffman) simply tower. There is no way of telling a boy's height either from his age or his family or geographical background. Later on this trip, when I encounter some fourteen-year old female pupils, I make the same observation (if anything, and bearing in mind that I met only a small group, the girls were much more of a uniform height but none of them could have been described in Australia or England as unusually short for their age).

On a previous visit, I had been shown over the College campus and visited the cafeteria just before lunch; there were several hundred steel bowls (Koreans favour steel cutlery in contrast to pottery and bamboo in China or Japan) filled with rice, an egg, some meat and kimchi. In volume, it was greater than a typical set lunch (teishoku) in a Japanese restaurant for office workers. So, given that these young people were born during the famine years, many of them show no sign whatsoever of long-term impacts. One thing which does seem absent from the diet, however, is high volumes of sugar. I often was given biscuits with morning and afternoon tea by Mrs. Kim (along with her duties in the College, she was assigned to look after me during teaching breaks) but these were originated mainly from Singapore and Malaysia and I did not see other teachers or students hungering for them. I did observe cans of fizzy drinks for sale in the many roadside stalls but, again, they did not seem universally popular (in summer, children prefer iced lollies of various fruit flavours). The result of this relative absence of chocolates, candies, cookies and sugared drinks is that, despite the amount of food available to these children, I never saw any youth who could even remotely be described as obese. Having said that, one boy did describe his class monitor to me as 'fat' which took me back slightly; he was the tallest boy in the class, well above the height of his female teacher, with the build of a wrestler but with the gentleness of a botanist (he was quite hopeless at catching the ball when we experimented with cricket one afternoon, much to his dismay and perhaps even to the detriment of his authority as monitor). Also, one of the female English teachers habitually referred to herself as fat – "I love to eat anything and everything!" she would tell me with a huge laugh – but, in my eyes, she was just a big, warm personality in a solidly-built frame.

For the pupils, the day begins early and ends late. A fleet of school buses collects them from all over the city around 7am – it can take up to an hour to reach the school gates - and takes them home around 6pm. Classes start from 8.30am, last for forty-five minutes, and formally end about 3pm; informal classes or one-on-one music or other lessons fill out the afternoon. Those dependent on the school bus either have extra tuition or stay on in their classrooms and start on their homework. All the pupils with whom I spoke said that they went to bed around 10pm so their time actually at home is quite short: after returning perhaps at 7pm, having the evening meal, more homework, and watching TV, the evening quickly is done. One thing which they did tell me often, however, is that they feel the school and its staff exist just for them; that the school is their domain and that they enjoy being there (in the long vacation some go back to school for extra lessons). As a teacher, this was good to hear.

The College itself is made up of three major teaching areas, plus a dormitory block for those pupils recruited from beyond Pyongyang. A sand and stone sports 'field' is on a slight ridge above the main building and is always occupied by boys playing either soccer or basketball. Girls tend to use the area around the new netball court, protected from the elements by the walls of the existing buildings which surround it on four sides. There, they play various forms of catch-ball during the breaks.

The central building of the College in west Pyongyang

There is a morning break of about fifteen minutes. Lunch is from 1pm to 2pm. The end of each lesson is announced by a snippet of recorded music, a gentle, lilting tune which, I was told by a colleague, is meant to be uplifting but which I occasionally mocked as a lullaby putting me to sleep. During the breaks, some children go out to play (boys usually form a group and practice football skills, for example, keeping a small ball or even piece of wood in the air), others engage in sweeping and mopping the school buildings. I have heard foreign commentators dismiss this latter kind of activity as drudgery, a meaningless task to give people the impression of work. If so, it is no different to the kind of sweeping and cleaning that is seen as virtuous and meditative in Buddhist temples (or the monasteries of medieval Europe), or indeed the same thing which is one of the most common features of private and public life in Japan.

One distinction of the College is that it has a high profile in the world of the arts. Among its graduates are some of Korea's most famous singers and dancers (my constant companion, Mrs. Kim, formerly was a dancer in a troupe and this connection to the arts may be why she joined the school's administration). One consequence of this is that, in the corridors, one frequently passes groups of older teenage girls specialising in dance; tall, slim, heads held high, prancing like proud ponies rather than walking like mere mortals. One also hears beautiful singing echoing through those same corridors, mostly in the afternoon when the regular lessons are over. When I am waiting in the central meeting room, which doubles as my informal classroom in the main building, I often sit back and close my eyes, just listening to the soaring voices echoing along the walls.

The City

The College is in the outer west of Pyongyang city, about twenty minutes' drive from the centre. The city itself has somewhere between two and three million people or easily ten percent of the entire population of the North. Across the city, there are extensive apartment blocks, uniform in size as in many countries but some of different designs and colours, often brightened by flowers in window-boxes (I never saw laundry drying on apartment balconies as is the norm in Japan). The skyline is relatively low, pierced only by the twin towers of the deluxe Koryo Hotel and the space-age rocket-shape of the enormous (and enormously ugly to my mind), still incomplete Ryugyong Hotel. Monuments and statues are mainly along the banks of the Taedong River (as wide as the Thames and taken over by pleasure boats in summer) and in the hill-side parks.

The 'rocket ship' Ryugyong Hotel intrudes on a park by the Potong River

The entire urban landscape of the North, as in wartime Japan, was erased by US bombers in the Korean War so there is nothing of even modest antiquity; everything had to be built or rebuilt from the late 1950s so, in 2011-12, there are massive renovation and reconstruction projects as the city as a whole begins to feel and show its age. The streets are usually broad, increasingly busy with vehicles at rush hours and far less so during the day, and lined with shops. These range from medium to large department stores to more specialist dealers. The most common types of shops are restaurants, including a few fast-food places, hairdressers (always busiest on Sundays) and those selling clothing. There are also quite a few photographers as, though many people in Pyongyang have their own digital cameras, special portrait photos are still desired for special occasions. Sunday is the major day for shopping because that is when parents and schoolchildren are both free. A subway rail system connects large parts of the city; trams and buses serve the rest. There are a few taxis visible on the streets but people are both used to, and comfortable with, walking distances of forty minutes or so. A good, strong pair of walking shoes is preferred to the costs and ostentation of a taxi.

In a book from 2005, *North Korea: The Paranoid Peninsula - A Modern History*, one Western analyst wrote that 'Shopping is an as-and-when activity in Pyongyang If a shop has stock, then returning later is not an option as it will be sold out.' I can only wonder if the author has ever been in Pyongyang (he seems to rely mainly on statements from defectors and refugees, and to picturing a world which, if it ever existed, belongs only in the most difficult years of the 1990s). Of the many stores that I have entered, from most of the department stores to tiny neighbourhood kiosks, there has never been an empty shelf. Return the next day and the shelves are still full. It is not a capitalist society – a stunningly obvious comment but one which bears repeating (if only because of the common wisdom abroad that Koreans are poor when what is actually meant is that they accumulate fewer consumer goods) - people are not consumers first and workers second. Also, they are not bombarded at every turn of their heads by advertising (it is said that in the US nowadays, an average citizen is hit by over 3,000 adverts daily – no wonder people look so tired). The rush to accumulate 'stuff', therefore, is not a natural part of life. Having said that, women clearly enjoy shopping for clothes and shoes as well as for 'accessories' such as bracelets or necklaces but they take their time, choose carefully, and make their own decisions. The result is that many women, especially those in their thirties and forties, dress elegantly or colourfully or both. At the

College, for example, Mrs. Kim always dresses smartly; on one occasion, seeing her in an ankle-length black coat with fur collar, I likened her to a Russian countess; the next day, in a bright-coloured, well-cut skirt suit, I told her she reminded me of a Parisian model (of the Christian Dior era rather than that of Jean-Paul Gaultier). She just smiled. The traditional women's costume of Korea, worn widely in the North, is a rainbow mix of colours and there is none of that timidity about wearing bright hues which one sees among middle-aged women in some countries.

Migyong

How can one not like the author Kurt Vonnegut? Late in life, this always inventive writer of alternative, sometimes absurdist, worlds and worldviews wrote about how he rejected calls from his acquaintances to conduct his life entirely by fax and email. No, he insisted, he wanted to take his manuscripts and correspondence down to his neighbourhood post office. He wanted to be among a crowd of people, to see old and new faces. In particular, he wanted to see the woman behind the desk, to see what she was wearing today, how she had done her hair, exchange a few pleasantries with her, and then return home loaded with these simple but very human gifts. Whatever anyone may tell you, he was saying, the human is a social, a communal, being. How right he was. Why do you think solitary confinement is used as a form of torture? For a man, the greatest pleasure in being, the most beautiful sight for the eyes and the heart, is not a sunset or a mountain landscape; surpassing all is the face of a woman. Venture into the street of any country in the world (even one where only the eyes of a woman are visible) and you are surrounded, freely and without condition, by beauty, not as two-dimensional images in weary poses on the internet, but in pulsating life. Venture into

Room 4 of Chongnyon Hotel and, once upon a time, you would have been enveloped by the beauty of one woman in particular: her name is Migyong.

Migyong is of small to medium height, slim, with the easy grace of someone much younger than her thirty years (she was a dancer in her youth). Her short hair, a popular Louise Brooks-style bob, swings in rhythm with her body as she walks, and her round, soft face reminds me of the American actress Sally Field. Migyong was one of the waitresses in Room 4. This is the dining room reserved for non-Korean guests. In practice, this means Chinese visitors who make up the overwhelming majority of tourists and businessmen in Pyongyang. Thus, Migyong and the other waitresses in Room 4 are trained to speak Chinese. Unlike the other women, however, both at Chongnyon and at some of the other hotels I have used in Pyongyang, Migyong was not in the least fazed by the appearance of a solitary Englishman.

After long experience in Japan, I often enter a restaurant in that country expecting one of two responses; either the staff will recognise as I scan the menu that I speak and read Japanese or, as still frequently happens, they will shut their ears to whatever I, the foreigner, say and assume there can be no possibility of our ever understanding each other. Given my limited understanding of Korean, the latter response always seems more likely, even inevitable, when I'm in Pyongyang. With Migyong, however, from the very first moment we met she was determined to work as hard as necessary to overcome all the many hurdles and obstacles to communication. With the patience of a primary schoolteacher, she instructed me every day on the correct pronunciation or choice of word of whatever I was trying to say to her. These were 'classes' to relish.

Her patience and generosity did not end there. During my first stay at the hotel in winter 2010, I was feeling the effects of the demands of the job, the different diet, and, overlaying everything, the onset of a really heavy chill (even though I had yet to encounter Ms. Pak and the café). After a sleepless night tossing with fever, I managed to make my way down to Room 4 for breakfast but did so without a shred of appetite. The usual bright smile of welcome from Migyong was quickly replaced by concern. She brought me the lightest dish available but after no more than a single bite I suddenly felt terribly ill and, there and then, threw up violently and extensively. As this continued, Migyong was patting my back, trying to ease the literally gut-wrenching pain. Once it was over, she quietly brought me a warm towel, wiped the sweat from my face and brought me a cup of warm water. She then proceeded with equal calmness to remove the stained tablecloth.

From that day on, Migyong adopted me not only as her guest but also as her charge. She brought me Korean herbal medicine, she watched over my diet, she gave me a hot water bottle for the evening when the outside temperature dropped through the roof (and continued to the basement). Every time I rose from my chair in the dining room, she was there to assist me. She took such endless care of me that I began calling myself 'grandfather' in her presence; she would laugh and answer, 'No, not grandfather; just father'. One day, she showed me an old photo of her family; it showed her own father in youth as a tall, handsome man and her mother as a very pretty woman. She also showed me a photo of herself and the family on her eighteenth birthday. Shortly before it had been taken, she had danced in a stage production of *Arirang*, the single most popular and romantic tale in Korea. The head of the country, Kim Jong'il, had attended the performance and, both as tribute to her dancing and in celebration of her birthday, had sent her a present of fine clothing; the box was in the foreground of the photo. That was Migyong; without even trying, and even from distance, she could enchant anyone, even the most powerful man in the country.

So, now I am back heading towards Room 4. Dinner in the hotel starts from 7pm and I would have been here on the dot but, it is the first evening of my stay and I have been talking longer than I intended with Manager Kim about our plans over the next few weeks; this means I enter Room 4 about 7.15. As I open the big, heavy wooden doors, and look into the large, round room lit by a huge glass chandelier, I see two Chinese men at a table to the right and, crossing the floor towards them, is our waitress for the evening. It is Migyong. She turns to greet this new guest at the doorway, that instinctive, unconditional smile of welcome already in place. Then she recognises me and the smile becomes even more wonderful; for the briefest of moments, she halts her progress and nods in my direction. Professional as always, she then hurries to the waiting diners. The two men are on the same floor as I and we met earlier while waiting for the lift (there is usually only one of the two lifts with power and so, in a thirty-storey hotel, one has time to make many new friends). They are gentle and kindly people in their mid-thirties; I take them for businessmen or technicians rather than tourists. They are smiling too; they have noticed Migyong's reaction. I sit down at the neighbouring table and wait my turn. It is good to be back in Room 4.

On my previous visit, I had brought small gifts for each of the women who had made my stay, both at the hotel and in the schools, so pleasant and so successful. These were necklaces of various stones such as a small opal, not expensive or opulent but, in keeping with what I see as Korean ideas about jewellery, quietly attractive. Receiving hers, Mrs. Kim at the

College had asked me shyly, 'Did you think of me when you bought this?' I assured her that I had chosen it solely with her in mind. When I gave Migyong her present, however, first she had said that she could not accept it because it was too much; she was only doing her job, she insisted, in looking after me. I countered that she did her job so well that I believed she deserved some special recognition and, in the absence of anything more imaginative on my part, this was what I had chosen. After lengthy protest, she finally capitulated, took the necklace, looked at it, and then asked: 'Is it gold?' I had to laugh; it was an entirely unexpected question. But then it may be that she had never received a gift of gold before and so it was something very special to her. To my regret, I had no definite answer; I certainly thought the chain was gold but it could easily have been gold-plated. I privately resolved to bring her a small present with a gold hallmark next time.

Now, having delivered their order, Migyong leaves the two Chinese guests to their meal and their conversation. She approaches me with that smile that would melt an Arctic glazier, and asks me in a great flurry of questions, when did I arrive, am I taking care of myself, and how long will I stay? Over the course of the evening, she comes back to talk whenever the opportunity arises. In time, the two others leave and politely say goodbye to her and to me. Once my meal is done and we are alone, I put a small case on the table. She looks at it and then at me, waiting for an explanation. I remind her of our last parting. Then I remind her of her disappointment that my thank you gift had not been gold. She protests that she had not been disappointed and she apologises profusely for having given me that impression. She now further insists that she cannot possibly accept a second gift but I explain that this is really a substitute for the first failed offering rather than a second one. Well, arguing is at least one way to improve my Korean language skills but I think Migyong takes pity on my limitations this evening and finally accepts the antique gold chain purchased in England just so I can stop flicking through the dictionary in search of all the words I need to make my case. As she puts it on, she continues to tell me that she is just doing her job, but I can see also that she is pleased.

It is then she tells me that we will not meet again after this trip. As she had intimated on an earlier visit, she has married one of her hotel co-workers in a low-key ceremony at home just a couple of months earlier and will soon quit her job in order to become a housewife and mother. I am delighted for her, and sad for myself.

The *Joie de Vivre* of Manager Kim

Having written at some length about a special woman, it is only appropriate that I should comment further on Manager Kim here. He was, and is, a man with several missions. One of them, rarely out of his mind, is to develop the best educational and cultural facilities for the schools which he manages. This involves frequent trips to China in search of help, information, and teaching materials. He tells me also that he has often represented the North at educational conferences internationally, though he remembers with greatest fondness his times in France and Germany (but also what appears to have been more of a Cossack-style hunting and drinking trip to the Russian Far East). He is quite the gourmand and enjoys both fine food and fine liquor. In Pyongyang, he is quick to praise good cuisine and good wine or beer, and equally quick to express disapproval when he feels the standards have fallen. Where he is resolutely and unconditionally positive and appreciative, however, is on the topic of women. He simply adores all women. On one occasion, we were in the hotel elevator together and there were about four women in between us. Manager Kim smiled and said to me in English, across their heads, 'Such beautiful ladies!' Privately, I thought that, with the best will in the world, these women could only be described as middle-aged and plain but I smiled back and nodded. In coffee shops and restaurants, Manager Kim would always, without fail, engage the waitresses in conversation, almost from the moment we sat down. They all seemed to take it in good spirits. In fact, I saw this engagement between waitresses and male customers across Pyongyang and in the other cities I visited on an earlier trip. It was another contrast with Japan where, unless the customers are long-term regulars, it is rare for a conversation to strike up and waitresses often seem to be aiming for invisibility.

On each of my trips, Manager Kim always arranged one special dinner at the Chongnyon Hotel for Teacher Kim and I. It was his way of saying a personal 'thank you', to me for coming a few thousand miles and having a busman's holiday, and to Teacher Kim for all the headaches (hence, all the cigarettes) that he suffered spending all day in my company and speaking almost nothing but English. Under normal circumstances, my two companions took breakfast and dinner in the dining room reserved for Korean guests so, apart from lunch (when Manager Kim was always busy elsewhere), we only relaxed together at the coffee shop immediately after returning to the hotel around 6pm, or sometimes at lunch in the city on Sundays. Thus, I looked forward to these special dinners.

On my previous trip, Manager Kim had ensured that Migyong was our waitress in the private dining room. It turned out that he and his wife once had an apartment in the same building as Migyong's family and that he knew her father. On this occasion also, it was Migyong whom he arranged to wait on us. Both of the Kims knew full well of my affection for her and so, with the four of us, it was a very pleasant and relaxed evening but tinged with regret at the knowledge that we would not do this again.

Teachers

While the College has a vast body of teachers, many of them specialise in one-to-one tuition in the arts, especially music. The English-language department has about twelve teachers, evenly divided between male and female. Their ages range from those in their twenties to those in their fifties. Apart from Teacher Kim who, temporarily, is relieved from teaching while he assists me but also works on drafting a new textbook, my closest and most frequent contacts are with Mrs. Kwak and Mrs. Song, both very attractive and intelligent people in their late thirties or early forties. The reason I see them each day is that they are responsible for many of the pupils given over briefly to my care. Mrs. Kwak is not tall but seems so because of her air of authority; she is always elegant and composed - a strong elder sister figure. Mrs. Song, with her slightly breathless voice and, occasionally, a look of sudden anxiety or sadness clouding her face, is a softer character, more of a younger sister in need of support even as she supports what she always terms 'my boys'.

As Kim is such a common surname and there are several teachers at the College called Kim, I try to distinguish them on any basis I can find. While my oldest friend and colleague monopolises the title 'Teacher' Kim, there is a younger man whom I often encounter. He is in his mid-thirties and with something of the look and all of the passion and intensity for his craft of a youthful Al Pacino. With steamroller logic, I dub him 'Young Teacher Kim'. The first time I met him was in a meeting I had with the assembled English-language teachers (in

Korea, departmental meetings are sometimes called 'friendship meetings'). With what, I later came to understand, was his typical approach, he was first off the block with a question and followed this up, almost instantly, with a barrage of several more. No other teacher had been so aggressive in his questioning – again, I later understood that this was not aggression, it was merely unbridled enthusiasm – so I was briefly taken aback but, when he gave me so little time to answer his first question, I had spoken to him quite sharply, saying, 'When you ask me a question, listen to the answer!' For a moment, I wondered if I had lost him, either by offending him or by not matching his own volcanic energy. Fortunately, he reined in his enthusiasm (at least for about two minutes), although with visible reluctance. Once I got to understand him, however, I could have spoken with him for hours, such was his intensity but also his charm. He leaped on new discoveries with obvious delight. He always carried a notebook and, when he sat in on my classes, I always saw him taking extensive notes in microscopic letters. He was one of those real teachers who know that you should never miss the chance to be a student.

Young Teacher Kim often dropped by Mr. Bak's office in the morning before the start of lessons (Mr. Bak always waited at the entrance for my transport to arrive and, after shaking hands and wishing me well, abandoned his office to my use for the morning). One day early in this winter visit, he came loaded with questions about a talk he had had with an elderly American teacher some months before. The talk had clearly made a deep impression on him. Among the points which the American teacher had emphasised most forcefully was the idea that the teacher's appearance was critical to his success in the classroom. 'You should always be dressed formally in jacket and tie so that the pupils respect you,' he had advised. Young Teacher Kim noted that I rarely (well, once a year on average) wore a tie, only occasionally a formal jacket, and that, in the winter, I usually had a brightly coloured red scarf. When he mentioned the American teacher's advice to me, I had to reply that it seemed a highly conservative and old-fashioned attitude. Of the two finest teachers in my experience, one was a university departmental head and habitually wore a suit and tie, the other was a writer and college lecturer who never did. Content and attitude, I suggested, is far more important than appearance: what you say and how you say it to the pupils matters more than whatever decorates your neck. Young Teacher Kim then asked what, for me, was the single most effective attitude with which to approach a student. In reply, I gave him my personal motto on the goal of a teacher: 'inform, encourage, inspire'. Inform the student of the facts, rules, or methods needed to understand the topic and, more generally, to be a student; encourage the student by emphasising anything positive and either minimising or overcoming the errors and failures; inspire the student by displaying your own enthusiasm for the job of learning. Naturally, instead of being overawed by these words of wisdom and accepting them as Moses might accept another commandment, Young Teacher Kim was not satisfied. What, he asked, if a student had special talents in one area but was weak or indifferent in another? Do you slow him down in order to strengthen the weakness, or do you drive full speed along the highway of his strengths and ignore the problems of his ignorance? It turned out that he had precisely such a student and was vexed about how best to help him. The student had imagination and could excel in creating short stories in English. In tests, however, his failings in grammar or his indifference to text-book memorization consistently let him down and he was in danger of failing the course, with disastrous consequences for his educational future.. All I could suggest was that Young Kim speak to the student privately and explain the situation clearly; in order to protect his imagination, he had to do the dull spadework of learning 'the basics' and passing what, to him, seemed like stilted exams. It was a limited challenge but the rewards, in terms of licence to continue doing what he enjoyed, were too great to risk. It came as no surprise to me when Young Teacher Kim said that this was exactly what he was now doing with the boy. He was, and is, an excellent teacher, albeit one perpetually frustrated by his belief that there must always be a better way to teach.

During my stays, I normally have a couple of 'friendship meetings' with the cohort of English-language teachers. These usually take place late in the afternoon at the conclusion of all the classes. Depending on who is present, these meetings can be up and down. On occasion, especially when Young Teacher Kim is absent or delayed, I have felt myself dragged into the quicksand of suffocating trivia, trying desperately to answer a question such as 'what is the difference between 'someone' and 'somebody', or 'which is correct – lift or elevator?' Usually, I answer that there is no difference; it is merely a matter of personal choice but I can always see that this does not satisfy my interrogator (the oldest of the female teachers is my constant bugbear in this respect). At the other end of the scale are the questions of Young Teacher Kim. On this trip, he wants to use the meeting to expand on our earlier chat and discuss ways of motivating a class to learn a language, a subject which, after all, is not receptive to reason and can only be learned through constant, unyielding determination (on a previous visit, I had tried to ease Mrs. Song's frustration by comparing her job, hamstrung with no direct access to the English-speaking world, to teaching children how to swim without water). Now he wants to see if I have a constant, underlying method to my teaching. This is something which interests all the teachers – they always ask me to bring books on the latest methods for teaching language - so I am happy to speak about it (especially if it means I can use it to avoid questions on 'somebody' and 'someone'). I say to him that, if I were able, I would like to start every class with something short and dynamic, preferably humorous also, so that the levels of comfort and energy in the class are bubbling from the start. Sometimes, I would try to maintain those levels throughout the class; other times, I would aim for a quieter period about half-way through before, once again, trying to raise the levels at the end. As a general approach, I think the aim is for the lesson to end with the student excited and the teacher exhausted. Then I would feel that my job was done. I have to qualify this, of course, by adding that I am in a unique position compared to him and the others: not only am I working in my own language and therefore freed from the effort of translation, I am attached to the schools in Pyongyang only for short bursts during the year. I admit freely that if I were to work long-term at the College, it would physically be impossible to maintain the investment of energy that he and the others have seen from me.

A Friendship Meeting, taken over as usual by Young Teacher Kim (far left)

At these Friendship Meetings, it seemed that I regularly managed to disappoint Mrs. Kwak. This was not something I intended; she had the most complete, indeed almost perfect, understanding of the English language among all the teachers I met in Korea; she also was the one who addressed me in the most natural and kindly manner by my first name and, in so doing, made me feel genuinely welcome. She could also stand up for herself admirably; if she believed something to be the case, she could be formidable in argument. I was told that she was a firm and demanding teacher but I also saw how committed she was to the welfare of her pupils.

The manner in which I disappointed her was in noting the changes in contemporary spoken and written English, changes brought about by technology and also by shifting attitudes among the youth of different nations. This revolved in large part around the practice of texting and also the impetus towards the kind of sound-bite style of 'conversation' or the twittering which now is known as tweeting. On hearing about these trends, Mrs. Kwak wondered anxiously what would happen to what she understood as standard English; could it survive this primitivization? I attempted to assure her that, at present, the trends which worried her remained in the minority and that, moreover, each generation invented its own terms and phrases in order to separate itself from its elders. In that sense, what was happening in some ways was not new (the resuscitation in recent years of the term 'cool', for example, no doubt gladdens the hearts of those who were young in the fifties). I did also stress, however, that all languages are living and evolving creations, and they evolve in the hands of their practitioners. To attempt to block this is no more likely to succeed than King Canute holding back the waves. I could see, however, that she was truly disturbed at the prospect that all she had learned, and all she had to teach, would somehow become redundant; in fact, was already becoming redundant. I tried to console her by adding that, if standard English were to be subsumed by the waves of txtspeak and tweeting, then I too would join her in being 'redundant' but that we could console ourselves by engaging in the most eloquent discussions whenever we met. She certainly had the ability to do that. I regret to say, however, that I never really convinced her and, like many of her generation in England itself, she remains anxious about the future of English.

Back In Class

It was clear from all the classes that I taught that the pupils are enormously interested in the unusual. In particular, they love mysteries, explorers and discoveries. Indeed, many of them told me in our informal conversations after class that their favourite reading was detective fiction. Popular among the many authors or fictional detectives are Sherlock Holmes and the works of Edgar Allan Poe (Teacher Kim had read Tintin in his youth and, on this trip, I bring a few pages of Tintin for reading and understanding practice in class). They also love to learn about the universe; stories set on the moon or other planets were a common choice whenever I asked them to invent a tale either in class or for homework. Equally, natural phenomena like volcanoes and hurricanes excite their interest, as do strange creatures. One of the most popular destinations for young people at the weekend is Pyongyang Zoo (apparently, there once was a kangaroo at the Zoo).

Realising all of this, I always bring with me a few unusual objects to show the students. These have included an example of Australian native art, with its distinctive style of composing a scene; photos of some of the cuter Australian animals (inevitably, the kangaroo and koala but also the rotund and chirpy kookaburra bird); and Australian banknotes with what may be their unique feature, a transparent window in the corner to deter forgers.

The banknotes also helped me to engage the pupils in a talk about heroes; Australian notes depict two prominent men and women, usually those who have contributed to society in some manner. I explained something about these people and then told the class about my own heroes, especially Martin Luther King Jr whose ability to organise and inspire others solely through his determination and speech, and without recourse to money or violence, remains matched only by his own role-model, and another of my heroes, Gandhi. I did also add that a third, slightly less famous, hero to me was my father. His early life had been a trial of fire following the deaths of his parents while he was still a child. As a result, he was already working at several jobs before his mid-teens but, through an absolute determination never to rely on others and to make his own way up, he ultimately became the managing director of a major firm in the hard man's world of the construction industry. The boys seemed to enjoy hearing about something so personal but, when I asked them about their own heroes (and also asked them on this occasion to exclude the leader of the country and present father-figure, Kim Jong'il), many of them chose their mothers. What seemed to run through each of their stories was the way in which their mothers went to any length to protect and support them (bringing a forgotten lunchbox all the way to school was a recurring theme). It seems that Korean fathers maintain the traditional attitude in East Asia of being a more remote parent; problems with homework, school or life in general are solved by the mother. The other popular choice of hero was the boy's teacher, irrespective of whether the teacher was male or female. The explanation, as with mothers, was the way in which the teacher obviously and endlessly cared for the welfare of the pupils. Finally, of course, there was the choice of a great sportsman as hero; here, the name of the Barcelona team footballer Lionel Messi came up time and again (the boys often told me they watched football matches from Europe). It was his combination of mastery of the ball allied to exceptional modesty which seemed most to impress these boys.

Only later did it occur to me that virtually no boy chose a soldier for his hero. A few of the boys had fathers in the army but this often resulted only in long periods of separation. Further, when we spoke about future careers, just a single boy declared that he was going to be an army officer; almost all said that they hoped for a job in computing, a couple wanted to be teachers, and one, a small, angel-faced boy called Song, wanted to be a singer (I later gave him an Irish whistle so he could make his own music and Mr. Bak, the trained engineer-turned-English departmental head, surprised us all by taking it and dashing off what sounded to me like an authentic Irish jig). In retrospect, I noted also that the textbook we used had no reference that I can recall to the Korean armed forces or to any military hero (there is also virtually no mention of Kim Ilsung or his son, disappointing though that may be to those foreign observers who insist that North Korean education begins and ends with the leadership). The subject 'Revolutionary History', the history of the DPRK, commences from the fifth year of secondary schooling so that the pupils' understanding of the military and war comes mainly from movies, TV, and comics.

One thing that Kōichi in Beijing had asked me to investigate was the attitude of schoolchildren towards money. He assumed, quite reasonably, that the children must carry a small amount of cash for snacks or something similar. One day, as I was showing a group of boys the Australian banknotes, I asked them if they carried any Korean money. Their answer was, 'we are children; we have no use for money' (I heard exactly the same thing from a group of girls later on). Instead, they told me, if they wanted something, they would mention it to their parents; it was the parents who dealt with money. All of the pupils I taught appeared to have their own computer at home; that was their biggest desire in terms of commodities (they also regularly played video games on their PC, with FIFA's official football World Cup being the favourite). I saw plenty of digital cameras in their hands when we went on trips to various places. Many of them also seemed to have mobile 'phones. So it is certainly not the case that they are 'poor' in the key material goods of the moment. However, the difference clearly is that the young people of Pyongyang are not so affected by the dictates of fashion; they do not demand the latest version of whatever it may be and cast off last year's model. This makes them much more contented than youth I see in other countries. Since advertisers in the English-speaking world in the 1980s discovered what they called 'skippies' (school kids with purchasing power), the concept of childhood in places like America and Britain has changed radically and the infiltration of consumerism has risen enormously. The children of North Korea, it seems to me, remain better protected from such trends. The result, paradoxically, is that childhood lasts longer and yet the children themselves are far less 'childish'.

Textbooks

One of the strongest impressions which emerged from classes and informal conversations with the students is their sense of pride in their country. This perhaps seems odd and even rather pathetic when contrasted with the insistence in the Western and other media about the poverty of North Korea. A recurring jibe against the North is the suggestion that people locally describe it as 'paradise'. A memoir by a young man who fled the North at the height of the 1990s famine, for example, is mockingly titled *This is Paradise!* In response, I should add that no-one I have met in North Korea has ever used this term, though this is not to say that the government has never used it, nor have I seen it in any school textbook (here it is worth mentioning that in a recent survey of North Korean defectors living in the South, one-third stated they would return home if they could – a remarkable figure for a country supposedly living an Orwellian nightmare). Among the exercises, there is an occasional comment which compares the society of the North favourably to some other countries; this is mostly in terms of the relative lack of pollution and the greater care for those such as the aged. There is no self-deception, however, about the hurdles for the North, both in the present and in the future. Energy consumption is a major problem and everyone is reminded of this by the frequent power cuts. It is the very frequency of such problems, however, which seems to have diluted them as a political or social issue; they have become just a part of life. At the outset of this account, I quoted the great Roman Stoic philosopher, Seneca, on the value not of what one endures but, rather, the value of how one endures. It seems to me that, in understanding North Korea, it is essential to recognise that endurance of hardship is regarded as a right and natural way to live.

On my various trips, I have taught boys aged from 13 to 15. This means I have used volumes three to five of the English-language textbook which, I was told, is employed in all schools across the country. It was first published in 2003, again I was told, based on a text issued by Cambridge University Press. Teachers in the North seem to share the international belief that anything from Oxford or Cambridge must be good, and they view British English as somehow superior to American English. When I first asked my colleagues at both schools what gift they would value most, they all pleaded for a copy of the Encyclopaedia Britannica. As some of them said to me, 'all we want is knowledge!' In fairness, I should add that they said they would gladly accept an American equivalent if the Britannica were unavailable.

The format of the textbook is straightforward. There is a short essay, usually of about one page, on a particular issue. This is accompanied by questions to prompt thought and discussion. There follows a series of grammatical exercises, not necessarily related to the essay. Finally, there is a dialogue for practice in conversation. It is this last element of each unit that I thought always the weakest. Generally, the dialogue is between family members or friends and revolves around something utterly mundane or trivial such as a mother asking her children if they have eaten their breakfast, or a father looking for his glasses only to be told by his children that they are on his head (I am making this last one up but that's the kind of topic they use). I thought these pupils were unlikely ever to be in the situation of needing to use or understand this kind of conversation, and that it sits poorly with the informative and thought-provoking essays. For that reason, I have never used the set conversations but made up my own instead.

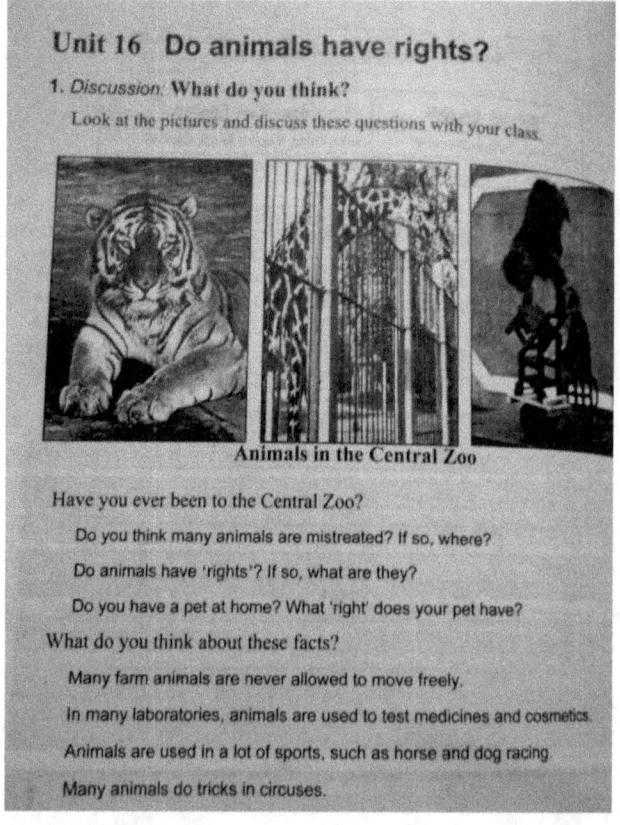

A typical opening page to a chapter in the English-language textbook

The essays broadly divide into two streams. One is focused on a particular country and its history. The other takes a universal question. Examples of the former include summary histories of Ireland, New Zealand, India, and South Africa. In each case, the emphasis is on the traumatic history of being colonised and abused yet, as with the Catholic Irish, the Maoris, the people of India, or the black peoples of South Africa, enduring and rediscovering pride in adversity, especially pride in one's language, customs, literature or music. In each of these essays, the basic historical facts cannot be doubted; what is being presented to the pupils is incontestable. Indeed, a Catholic Irish student reading the same text on Ireland as a boy or girl in Pyongyang could have no criticism of what was presented.

The more general essays are often about global problems, especially those of technology, energy reserves, and air pollution. Again, the facts and the debates are presented simply and clearly. If there is any bias, it is both partial and justifiable. For example, in a comment on capitalist societies, the text notes that older people are particularly at risk. It explains that this is because the fragmentation of society often leaves them isolated, lonely and afraid, not least that their pensions might not keep pace with the rising costs of energy, especially of heating in winter.

In May 2011, I was asked to proof-read and comment critically on the draft of a new English-language textbook. This was a joint project of the two schools at which I taught and was intended for publication in 2012. I learned later that it was aimed at their senior pupils, those aged 15 and 16, but the hope was that it would be adopted by other schools across the country later on. There were several remarkable things about this new textbook. One was the excellence of its construction; each text seemed to build logically on the other. Also, the language was virtually flawless in its grammar and choice of vocabulary. Finally, the essays for reading and discussion were right up-to-the-minute, many of them sourced from the internet and used because of the way they dealt with present-day issues of life and technology.

Other features of the draft included the absence of hostility towards any other country. In particular, there were many references to life in the U.S. but nothing that, as far as I could see, could even remotely be viewed as critical of America or Americans. The example that sticks most firmly to mind is an internet article titled 'Brother can you spare a dime for my Gucci bills'. The story in this was of a middle-class American woman who, despite having a good and well-paid job, found herself so heavily in debt she could not pay her bills. Almost as a joke, she decided to appeal through the internet for charity. So many people responded, however, because she made it completely clear that she was not trying to deceive anyone and she didn't use pictures of lame dogs or crying children to evoke sympathy. The textbook noted that there is a practice which has become known as cyber-begging, and also noted that the woman had received as much hate mail as she had received charity but, to the pupils using this text, the question was left entirely open: what do you think – was she acting unethically or was she being creative? So, no criticism of American society, either as weak and debt-ridden, or soft and sentimental; just, here it is, make up your own mind.

In a similar vein, the references to Japanese examples of modern life were devoid of hostility; a remarkable thing in a country which, both North and South, was treated with extreme racist contempt and brutality over the colonial era. In fact, a South Korean historian wrote an article some years ago about rumours in Korea during World War 2 concerning the Japanese overlords. One of the rumours he cited from the 1940s warned that the Japanese military was rounding up Korean girls, not for sexual exploitation but in order to drain their bodies of chemicals needed for the war effort. It may be that there isn't a shred of scientific logic in the rumour but that is completely beside the point. It shows, accurately, that Koreans then and later believed the Japanese viewed them as sub-human, and treated them with less respect than they granted an animal.

In the draft textbook, one of the extended essays sourced from the internet was about the Japanese inventor of the karaoke machine. The essay was reproduced faithfully from its source, showing the inventor as a man who was happy to have given pleasure to millions and unconcerned that, in failing to copyright his invention, he had missed his chance to become as rich as Croesus. In short, he was a good and generous man; a good and generous <u>Japanese</u> man. This was a possibility that one rarely heard in North Korea, and that is precisely what made its appearance in this teaching resource so very welcome.

One thing about the draft textbook (now in use) is that its attitude to the outside world – asking questions, wanting to know - is in such stark contrast to the North's official English-language media, especially the Korea Central News Agency or KCNA. It is the KCNA which usually is cited by Western press and T.V. to show the North as unrelentingly bellicose and volatile, locked in a Cold War time-warp. Indeed, a senior and sympathetic analyst of North Korean affairs from New Zealand, Dr. Tim Beal, gave an interview not long ago to the *Pyongyang Times* in which he warned that the KCNA's sometimes hysterical and often outdated rhetoric on American and Japanese 'imperialism' served only to damage the North's standing in the world. In conversation with a young official, I went further and suggested that it be renamed the Korea Central Information Agency, or K-CIA, on the grounds that it clearly was working in concert with the American CIA and zealously handing over propaganda bullets to the North's enemies. The official smiled and answered diplomatically that there was an older generation in Pyongyang which had to pass on before some things could change.

Problem Kids

In each of the schools where I worked, I was given responsibility for one hundred children per visit. Naturally, not every one of them was comfortable and confident in dealing with a foreign language non-stop for forty-five minutes every day. A few of them looked at me nervously whenever I asked a question, one or two of them kept their heads down relentlessly. Usually, I would deliberately put a question to one of these boys, asking them to stand with me, and encouraging them at least to try. What I noticed on such occasions was that the others in the class would whisper out clues to the answer; the group protected its own. At the College, there was only one boy whom I never seemed able to reach. He was tall and well-built but he had not the slightest confidence when it came to speaking English. When I asked him a question, he just looked desperately to his neighbour and never made an attempt of his own to deal with the problem. Whenever I was addressing the class as a whole, I could see from his lack of facial response that he was entirely adrift in his own universe. On one day, at the teacher's request, I gave a test to each of the boys; this was a two-minute monologue on 'a day in the life of...' This boy chose to talk about a football player but much of the vocabulary came from the textbook (if I remember correctly, there was a section which described a match between Manchester United and maybe Liverpool). So, when pushed and with no escape, he could just scrape by but it was a disappointment to me that I could not reach him better.

Another student was something of a puzzle. For much of my stay in November-December 2011, he was coughing and spluttering through each class. I often asked him if he were alright and shouldn't he really be resting at home. No, he insisted, it was no problem, and so he continued to turn up every day, and cough and splutter through the lesson. On the day of the test, late in the visit, I called him to the front of the class when it was his turn. In the meekest of voices, he explained that he was not prepared. Teacher Kim was sitting beside me, checking my mark for each boy's performance (he did not disagree with a single mark I gave). He was surprised at this boy's failure and told him that we had reserved an extra period in the afternoon for any boy whom we could not hear in the morning. It was essential, therefore, that he appear at this time and with no further excuse. Come the afternoon, however, we were sitting and waiting for this boy, the only one who had let himself down in the morning. Still he did not show. Mrs. Kwak, who had joined us and was talking over the results, went in search of him. About ten minutes later, she returned with her prisoner who apologised again for his non-appearance. Despite everything, he did not, or could not, explain why he was acting the way he was (Mrs. Kwak told me later that there must be some special reason because he, along with all of the boys, she insisted, genuinely looked forward to my classes and he would not behave like this without a reason). What struck me is that neither of the teachers took a hard-line with this boy; there was no threat of punishment and neither of them interrogated him. When we finally heard his piece, it was good - grammatically sound and reasonably well put together - so I gave it a mark on its merits and added only a small penalty for all the trouble we had experienced with him. The irony of all this is that, the following day, the boy's cough seemed to have disappeared and, in its place, he was just bubbling and chuckling with laughter; every time I or one of the class said something even remotely amusing, I could hear him guffawing. It was clear that he actually understood everything that was being said (the laughs were all in the right place and all at the right level of hilarity). On this evidence, he had a claim to being the best student of English in the entire school. Why we had been forced to 'sheepdog' him into doing the test, however, was forever to remain a mystery.

There was a third 'problem kid' of sorts. It was me. Apparently, some of the teachers were worried that my lessons were too improvised and that the textbook was being forgotten. After a warning hint from Manager Kim (which I rebutted on the grounds that the pupils could use the textbook any time but I was there to engage them just for short periods), the big guns appeared in the form of Mr. Goh, the administrator responsible for both of the schools where I worked. Mr. Goh was immensely tall, easily 6' 4", thin and with a severe face, tinted glasses, and several gold teeth which made him look like the ideal Bond villain, a cross between Dr. No and Jaws. He was, of course, also a charming man, committed to teaching, easily approachable, and quick to smile. He had been the first one, a year before, to suggest I take on a class of girls now that I had won over the boys; 'That will be the real challenge!' he had said to me with a laugh. Now he came to the school to talk to me about the textbook. It was, he explained, a legal responsibility of the schools to work through the curriculum. I repeated my arguments earlier to Manager Kim. He listened, obviously in some discomfort about the position in which I was placing him. The textbook, I suggested, was like dry land; the children were in need of water to swim with their language skills, and only through extensive engagement in listening and responding in natural conversation could they improve quickly on these skills. Teacher Kim confirmed that he could see rapid progress among many of the students but Mr. Goh still had his legal responsibility in mind. I decided it was time to make a concession and agreed that I would employ the textbook in more lessons. His relief was obvious; the gold-toothed smile was back.

Two Transactions

One day, Teacher Kim and I took our usual walk after lunch and I was reminded that to some people I may be, if not an intruder, at least an alien and unsettling presence. We walked along the road past the school and towards the vast Mangyongdae Children's Palace, the great building devoted to teaching and training children of all ages in music and performance. I had visited the Palace as a tourist on my first visit and been shown some of the rooms where children practised piano, dance and so on. Today was a fine if chilly day and so I suggested we keep walking beyond or away from the Palace. On the other side of the road there were various shops. I asked Teacher Kim what the larger of these was selling and he said it was a tailor's. I was interested to see what kind of clothes it offered and said that I had always wanted to have a waistcoat made for me in Pyongyang. I suggested we go and have a look and then return to the school via the far side of the road. Teacher Kim, however, was most reluctant. He offered an array of reasons why we shouldn't; there was nothing to see, the shops would be closed for lunchtime etc. Naturally, I pressed further, completely unconvinced by these wafer-thin arguments. 'The people round here,' he finally admitted, 'are not used to seeing foreigners and they might be disturbed. You don't want to disturb them, do you?' he asked. I suggested that my presence, so clearly in his company, probably would not disturb anyone, and that it should be worth experimenting to see what, if any, reaction we got. The school was not far from Chongnyon Hotel and we had often walked around that heavily-populated area before (driving back from a different direction one day, I saw amid the row after row of apartment blocks the largest supermarket I had ever seen in Pyongyang and, to my surprise, it had a great neon sign in English, 'Supermarket' above its entrance). None of the adults there had ever given me more than a passing glance and it was only the very young children who would stare. However, Teacher Kim was all in favour of the quiet life and now resisted this venture into the unknown. As I really had no wish to disturb anyone, and certainly not to worry him, I let the matter drop. As we walked back, however, he asked: 'Do you really want a tailor-made waistcoat?' I considered: what had been a spur-of-the-moment idea was, on reflection, rather attractive. I thought of my debonair colleague from the other school, Teacher Ham, always nattily dressed in a light suit, tie and waistcoat. 'Yes,' I replied, 'I really would.' As reward for my conciliatory attitude, he promised to call the tailor's we had passed, so near and yet so far, and see what could be done.

The next day, there was disappointing news. It was 8.20am and we were preparing in the staff room for the start of the day; this usually meant me just going through my opening lines while Teacher Kim called administration and checked which classroom we were to start with. 'The tailor's,' he said. 'It only makes women's clothes. We will have to try elsewhere. Manager Kim is checking for you.' By now, my mind was on teaching, not on waistcoats, so I made no comment. Later in the day, however, there was a surprise; Manager Kim had found that there was a tailor's in the hotel itself (as I discovered there was in other hotels). He had arranged for us to go along after teaching and discuss my needs in person.

Early in the evening, we returned to the hotel and went to the back rooms, past the billiards room, the karaoke and the barbers, and there was a sign I had not noticed before: 'yangbok'. It was the tailor's. When we entered, it was a largish room with a broad table and a sofa. The tailor turned out to be a handsome middle-aged woman, all business, and, with the briefest of greetings, she was at work with her tape-measure. She laughed, not unkindly, as I stood in the chilled room without jacket or sweater (she, of course, had a thick jacket on at all times) but, once all the figures were in her notebook, she simply asked me what shape and colour of wool I wanted. On the table, there was a pattern book and I found a page dedicated to waistcoats. I chose the style and colour I preferred. Having done this, she gave me an estimate and a quote. The price was half that I would pay in Australia and the first fitting could be in two days. I was so impressed with her efficiency that I asked her to make a second one for me and we left the fitting for the following week as I was due briefly to change hotels in a couple of days. Sure enough, when I returned the following week, the waistcoats were ready for fitting, the measurements and the cutting had been exact, and I was thoroughly pleased with the outcome of what had been just a playful thought a fortnight earlier. The tailor was also satisfied but she did not show much emotion; she was a professional and knew full well she had done a professional job. When I said that I liked them both, she simply said, 'Good. Then we'll see you again'.

Late in the Soviet Union, there was a popular saying which crystallised the cynicism of that particular failed system: 'they, the government, pretend to pay us and we, the workers, pretend to work'. The tailor, and all the teachers, waitresses, guides and others I have met in Pyongyang over the years are not pretending to work; they do their work and they do so with an obvious commitment both to the job and to their society. Foreign observers routinely label the North Korean system a failure and predict its collapse but to understand why it endures, one must also recognise that there are many who remain faithful to it and for whom it provides what they need; a sense of belonging and, yes, a sense of pride.

On the subject of money and transactions, clearly my salary was gauged to Australian dollar prices and was far in advance of Korean wages. As a result, it was tacitly understood among us that I would pay whenever we had a meal or a drink together. I never questioned nor complained about this because both Manager Kim and Teacher Kim were working non-stop to ease my stay. There was one time when we were in a restaurant having lunch on a Sunday and I left early because I was feeling shattered after catching one cold after another. I was sure that Manager Kim had offered to pay on this occasion but, as I got back to the hotel, I was no longer so certain. Later that afternoon, I asked him whether I had been muddled; he replied simply that he also could not remember and left it at that. Later that day, we were walking around the city centre and I suggested we go into one of the shops; it was full of food, drink, household goods and also small to large electronic appliances. As we were browsing, Teacher Kim mentioned to me quietly that it was Manager Kim's birthday the following day. Just at that moment, Manager Kim was caressing a bottle of Chivas Regal and saying, for all to hear, 'Yes, Chivas Regal – very good, very fine!' He then placed it back on the shelf and went to admire other whiskies and brandies. I took the hint, and took the bottle to the cash desk. This particular shop had a plentiful supply of euros so the exchange was quick and simple. As I looked up, there was Manager Kim standing by my side; I passed the bottle over to him – no fuss, as would have been the case in Japan, about wrapping on wrapping – and said, 'Happy birthday for tomorrow.' He accepted it graciously and gratefully. I would say our accounts were back in balance.

Excursions

I was in the classroom from 8.30am to 3pm six days a week and usually had another hour or two of informal classes daily. This is how I wanted it and I kept telling Teacher Kim and Manager Kim, whenever they said I should slow down or take a break that I was here to teach. Manager Kim did continue to press on me the value of taking a small group of pupils outside the school occasionally, as a break for all of us and to show them something different.

One of Manager Kim's suggestions was to visit Pyongyang Zoo but it was clear from the stories of the boys (and, later, girls) that they went to see the animals so often that I doubted it would be much of an excursion for them, or me.

One of my suggestions was to visit the rather grand automobile showroom next door to my hotel. The plan was to talk to the manager and hear about the progress of the company, the technology in the vehicle (which I understood to be sourced from the Italian giant, Fiat), and the prospects and problems for the Korean car industry in the future. Manager Kim promised to see what he could do but, the day after this conversation, he came back to me and explained that there was a problem. I waited, as usual. He had been to the showroom. But the boss apparently had said that he was interested only in speaking to those who wanted to buy his vehicles, not a bunch of kids who would only ask him a lot of needless questions about them. I did mention to Manager Kim that I thought this a short-sighted attitude; these boys of 14 might all be car-owners in another decade and, if I were running a commercial venture, I would want them to have a special fondness for my product from an early age. Still, I understood that the showroom was all about business today and not about education, or even business for tomorrow, so I dropped the idea (for this visit, at least – I have found that if you stick to something and refuse to take 'no' for an answer that problems can ultimately disappear in North Korea).

A roadside advertisement for Pyonghua Motors, one of North Korea's major vehicle manufacturers.

Among the places we did visit were two of the major museums in Pyongyang. One was an historical museum of ancient Korea, rich in artefacts but telling a sometimes unconvincing jingoistic story of early innovation; the other was a museum dedicated to the war of 1950-53. The latter has a simple central theme; it is that, in war, (North) Koreans are heroes and Americans are cowards. This is presented most obviously and dramatically in a vast theatre where a massive painted tableau revolves around the audience chamber. Depicted is one of the ground battles, and the key element among all of the fighting and carnage is an American general cowering behind a bush as a muscular young Korean hero towers triumphantly above him. Little is heard or seen of the South Koreans either here or throughout the displays. Yet, it was very rare among the people I met in Pyongyang to see or hear genuine hatred for anything American; that was reserved for the Japanese. Even in the Museum, there was no emphasis on war crimes or atrocities which might increase anti-Americanism. Instead, the emphasis was on the war as a military contest of material and spiritual resources in which, simply by surviving undefeated, the North could claim a great victory.

The visit to the War Museum reminds me of virtually the sole occasion where I was in direct conflict with one of the boys. The student in question was an endlessly smiling, endlessly involved and energetic young man whose bright personality and enthusiastic contribution to the lesson lifted my spirits every time I entered the room. If I asked a question of the class, he was always there offering an answer. In the competitive language games we played in class, he exuded enjoyment in the challenge, though he also relished (as did many of the other most advanced pupils) the chance to be, as we came to put it, 'crafty, sneaky, tricky,' in his questions for the other teams. Whenever I spoke privately to one of these teams and asked them what question they intended to pose, there was often one of the boys who almost rubbed his hands with glee at coming up with the most difficult, devious, or unpredictable question. He was one of those. He was also, however, a very handsome and gentle young man and I said to Teacher Kim once that I wished I could post this boy's photo on a Japanese website; the enchanted schoolgirls of Japan, the only dynamic force in that poor, exhausted country, would undoubtedly force the Japanese government to be much kinder in its attitudes towards the North.

Our moment of confrontation came in a class where, for whatever reason, I was explaining the different meanings of the word 'civil'. Among these, I mentioned also the idea of civil war and, as an example of this, said to the class, 'as in the Korean civil war'. Hearing this, the young man in the front row immediately shot up and called out, not aggressively but certainly with force; 'No, that was not a civil war; it was a war of aggression by the US against the Korean people!' This is the accepted view in North Korea and, as an historian, I can see how a case in defence of it can actually, and actually quite easily, be made. So, naturally, I did not attempt to 'correct' or change his position but, instead, told him and the class only that this phrase was commonly used in the English language about the war in Korea and that they should understand what it meant if they ever encountered it in a book or film. It was a useful moment to me; it impressed on me both the strength of this interpretation in the North but also the strength of the student who, putting aside his usual affability, was instantly ready to stand up for what he believed to be true.

'Tiger Killer'

This particular day I wanted to teach the boys about the idea of constantly giving oneself a challenge and never being satisfied with success. It is, I suppose, an invitation to life-long misery but also, perhaps, the best way to obtain the most from life. As prelude to the 'main course' of the lesson, I had two quotes which I put up on the board. The first was from Cicero, the Roman statesman and orator from the time of Julius Caesar, whose selected works I had brought with me as bedtime reading. In perhaps the best of his essays, written late in his life, he had expounded on old age and, in this, I had been struck by one sentence: 'I grow old learning new things.' It was such a simple, yet eloquent statement that I wanted to share it with the boys even if they were still far too young to appreciate it: a life of learning; that is what I wanted them to think about. The other was one of Nietzsche's most famous assertions: 'what does not kill me makes me stronger'. My purpose here was to encourage them also to be ambitious and adventurous rather than conservative and afraid. One example I used was that of exams. What was the personal benefit to them of taking exams? What could we learn about ourselves by taking an exam? It did not take long for some of these bright young men to see the point: we can discover our mistakes, they said. Then, I asked, what can we do? We can correct them, they said. Yes, of course. For that reason, I suggested, we should not fear a test or exam but treat it as an opportunity to see ourselves, our strengths and, more importantly, our weaknesses.

I then moved on to the broader topic of giving oneself a challenge. For this, I chose one boy in each of the classes, gesturing to him to stand and come and join me. Unconsciously, I probably chose more of the smaller boys to emphasise the point that was coming. In one of the most able classes, I chose a boy of slightly below average height whom I later took to calling 'Tiger Killer'. He had a perfectly round face, just like one of the cuddlier teddy bears, two small eyes, twinkling with intelligence and amusement, and the kind of broad smile that belongs to one of those 'smiley faces' that children love to draw at the end of letters. He also had the most perfect English pronunciation and intonation. I defy anyone to guess from speaking to him on the 'phone that he is not a native English speaker. Yet, he was from the most northernmost city in the DPRK so I could only assume that his sole exposure to English came after arriving at the school, where he boarded along with perhaps a couple of hundred other pupils from beyond Pyongyang. Put simply, he was a natural but I really liked his easy confidence and his quick wits so I knew that, in choosing him, I was certain to get my point over.

'Let's think of a challenge, boys,' I said. 'What kind of challenge could our young friend here give himself, really to test himself?' The class was waiting because they could sense I was ready with a suggestion. 'What about...', I paused, 'fighting a rabbit? Is that a good challenge?' I got the response I hoped for with howls of laughter across the room. I put one hand on 'Tiger Killer's shoulder and, with the other, traced the outline of a small, fluffy rabbit. The laughter, thankfully, continued. Tiger Killer was the perfect foil; he stood there impassively, just smiling calmly and waiting for his lines. 'What,' I continued, 'if he fought a tiger?' The boys roared again at the thought of their young classmate venturing into tiger country (a saying in nineteenth-century Korea was, 'for half the year, the Korean hunts the tiger; for the other half, the tiger hunts the Korean'). 'Would you', I turned to my accomplice, 'be willing to fight a tiger in order to challenge yourself?' He thought for a moment, then replied, 'Yes, I would be willing.' The boys continued to enjoy this prospect. 'What do you think will happen, boys, if our young friend challenges himself and fights a tiger?' I asked. 'He will be killed!' one shouted. 'He will be eaten by the tiger', another declared. 'Maybe he will live' a third offered. I seized on this. 'Yes, maybe he will live. And if he does live, do you think he will ever be afraid of anything?' No, they all agreed, he will not fear anything. 'So,' I asked, 'if the tiger does not kill him, he will be stronger, much stronger?' Everyone concurred. The boy stood there, calm and amused. 'Then, my young friend, what will you do tomorrow morning, before coming to school?' He smiled and stated in that mellifluous English of his, 'Tomorrow, I will fight a tiger!' The class just exploded with delight.

The next day, I wanted to introduce a different phrase, 'breaking news', in part to emphasise my point that language could be very strange. After all, how, or why, did news break instead of simply emerge or appear? After the usual greetings and telling the boys the outline of the class, I stopped in the middle of the room and asked, 'Did you hear the news this morning, boys?' They explained that the TV news appeared only in the evenings and that few, if any, of them listened to the radio so, no, they had not heard any big news that day. 'Well, boys, there is breaking news.' I indicated to them what was meant by 'breaking news' and put on my best 'serious' face. 'Yes, boys, there is breaking news; it comes from Pyongyang Zoo.' Some of the boys were listening seriously, some, on hearing the word 'zoo' had begun to suspect a joke. 'This morning, at 7.15 am, boys, the staff of the Zoo went to feed the tigers.' The class as a whole was now beginning to see what was coming. I walked up to 'Tiger Killer' and motioned for him to stand beside me. 'Yes, boys, the staff went to feed the tigers but, guess what - no tigers! Breaking news!' We were off and running again. I turned to 'Tiger Killer' and asked him, 'Did you go to the zoo this morning?' He smiled and said, 'I did.' 'So', I ventured, 'you can explain for us the mystery of the missing tigers. Did you kill the tigers of Pyongyang Zoo?' The class waited for the answer. 'No, I did not kill the tigers of Pyongyang Zoo', he announced. 'Breaking news, boys', I continued, emphasising the phrase we were using: 'The schoolboy known as Tiger Killer did not kill the tigers!'. With a broad smile, he declared, 'I released them from the zoo. They are now in the mountains'. It was a good answer. In one of the textbooks, there was a lesson on animals' rights in which the central question was, do you think animals have rights? It also allowed me to come back to the story in later days with questions such as, did he go to see them and how were they doing? For someone of just 14 to be that skilful in working a kind of double-act in a foreign language is quite something. Having said that, the nickname 'Tiger Killer' really took hold and, on at least one occasion, I heard the other boys refer to him not by his real name but as 'Tiger Killer'. I only hope his father did not follow suit.

Mansudae and the Arts

On one of our Saturday afternoons, Teachers Kim, Kwak and Song plus a group of about ten boys made a visit to the Mansudae Arts Studio, the major gallery and artistic workshop in the city. When we arrived, the power was off and the gallery space was pitch-black. The woman who was to show us around was waiting in the entrance, exchanged a few words with Manager Kim and then called out 'kapsida!' – 'Let's go' - as she headed off to another building. I decided not to follow and so the boys and other teachers also held back. I thought there was enough light from the entrance to view the paintings on the wall and that, if anything, the half-light actually added something to them by removing other distractions. Seeing what we were doing, the gallery assistants found a torch and followed us around. This also added to each of the paintings, framing and separating them from the others, giving us the chance really to focus on the individual subject. Overall, the three most popular and common types were: landscapes, usually of the mountains or coast; figurative of all kinds from workers to children and beyond; plus animals, almost entirely tigers and eagles (though in sculptures or woodwork, there were others such as turtles, rabbits etc.).

Three paintings stood out for me in this contemporary exhibition of well over fifty pieces. One was of a group of small children on and around a park bench. All were either playing or gazing at something marvellous but one girl alone was trying, and clearly failing miserably, to read a book; in frustration, she had clamped her hands to her ears and her expression of annoyance was perfectly captured. I liked it because of the humour with which it was composed, the small tragedy of life in a group which it showed, and the fact that it so clearly acknowledged that children in Korea were of different minds and personalities.

Another painting stood out because I found it rather repulsive. It was a portrait (head and torso) of the 21st century Korean young women, the 'modern girl' of Pyongyang. She was dressed in a light brown jacket with the requisite Kim Ilsung badge (a badge which I always think is very simply a mark of being Korean) but with bits of glitter and glitz attached to her pocket, wrist and neck. In the background, it is a spring day with trees glazed in rich greenery but she is entirely and exclusively engrossed in her mobile 'phone; nothing else exists for her beyond its tiny screen. I am still not sure whether the artist was celebrating the 'progress' of Korea – I am sure that is how many observers would see it – or condemning the narrowness of his subject's new world. That is what made the painting so interesting; it gave you the freedom to choose for yourself. As I recalled, the most common phrase in the school textbook was, 'what do you think?' So too was it here.

The third painting of special interest was of a group of workers heading for home at the day's end. The artists had focused also on their faces and torsos, all broad-shouldered, big-muscled workers with square faces and wide grins. There was an ebullience about the faces that I liked; instead of the usual cartoon features, these were all carefully detailed, each one completely different to the other. But what gave it a particular charm was that one of the group of men in the foreground was looking down as he paused to light his cigarette; it was a moment of absolute believability, that moment when leaving the factory, the mine or wherever, instead of singing revolutionary songs or shaking his fist at the 'imperialists', the working man rewards himself with a smoke and the anticipation of a glass of beer. I thought the scene could have come from anywhere, Pittsburgh or Glasgow just a few decades ago, or any place where men and women still work amid heat and dust and noise.

I spoke to the boys about my responses to these and other paintings. They also appreciated the humour of the frustrated girl child, and the variety of working men's faces; about the girl and her mobile phone, they were non-commital. It, or she, was now just part of the landscape of their lives; they neither reacted for nor against her. When I asked them for their favourites, however, there were two clear winners. One was of a tiger, drawn with impressive realism, staring back at the viewer with an expression which said 'go ahead - make your move'. I could see the skill of the artist but, as I told the group, I could never hang such a painting in my house because my wife would never dare enter the room! The other painting they all admired was easier to live with; it was a vast canvas, covering an entire wall, showing head on the sides of a mountain range. Again, it was depicted with such skill that you felt you were actually on the mountainside. It was this combination of accuracy and the spectacular beauty of the mountains, so often praised in Korean arts and literature, that enthralled both them and I.

Usually, I would buy a painting when I visited Mansudae because there was always something that caught my eye and which I wished to share with others overseas. On this occasion, I was told that all the paintings were to remain on exhibit for some time and, only after its finish, would they be priced and offered for sale. I knew I would return the following year so I was not too disappointed (on my next visit I bought the print of the little girl trying to read) but, so as not to leave empty-handed, I purchased a small embroidery or sué-girim of two birds on a branch, one looking disconsolate, the other looking at her (or him) with sympathy. Mrs. Song had recommended it to me as a character study in relationships – every marriage or partnership is like this - and I could see what she meant. I liked it as another example of people in North Korea thinking, feeling and acting just like anyone else.

T.V. , Film and Images

The colloquial name for television when I grew up in England was 'the idiot box'. A social history of Japanese television published a few years ago bears the title *A Nation of 100 Million Idiots* and I have frequently told my students in Australia that, after a few hours of watching Japanese TV, one loses the will to live (it really is that bad). In the U.S. the only program on the myriad channels I have ever been able to watch regularly is *The Simpsons* (here, I am reminded of the memoir by actor Sidney Poitier which begins with him going back and forth through all ninety-two channels and, on finding not one thing of interest, asking himself – 'what am I doing with my life?!'). Indeed, about four years ago, I did what every rational person in this situation can and should do; I switched off the TV at home. Since then, I have never felt the temptation to switch it back on. In North Korea, however, I felt I had to watch some TV in order to improve my understanding of the place and the people, especially of the young people whom I was there to help (at least I would be spared commercial advertising with all its sweaty desperation).

The students told me that they watched TV regularly in the evenings (broadcasts begin late in the afternoon except on Sunday when there is a full day's schedule). At this time, there were three channels; Pyongyang, Mansudae, and the Educational and Cultural Channel. In addition, there was a new cable channel which seemed at this early stage still to be limited to the Pyongyang region. One of the self-styled 'quality' English newspapers had insisted a few months earlier that North Korean TV broadcast only and exclusively two subjects; the Leader and the military. In the real world, as opposed to this Orwellian horror-fantasy world, the truth is completely different. On all the channels, there is a mixture of programmes, especially, music, movies, documentaries, and, most popular of all with teenage boys, cartoons and sport. North Korean news is naturally focused on domestic events and seems always to be reporting success and new ventures; a radical alternative to the incessant litany of murder, catastrophe and misery that dominates the news in the countries where I live. The news occasionally includes footage from other countries; I recall on my first visit in 2006 being surprised to see film of the British parliament and the violently hated prime minister of the time, Blair, taking a barrage of criticism from both the opposition parties and his own. In passing, it is worth noting that in the various hotels where I stayed, the TV sets in the room were tuned to Chinese channels and, in the more expensive establishments, to Russian, British (BBC World) and Middle Eastern news stations. It is entirely possible, therefore, that the cleaning or maintenance staff could see foreign programmes if they really wished to.

The style of news-reading often appears fixed and rigid in many countries. In some, there is a clear division of labour between a team of male and female readers; in others (CNN comes to mind) there is a rhythm of speech and a body language which instantly identifies the station. In North Korea, all the newsreaders I observed were female, middle-aged, and spoke in a declamatory voice which would not have been out of place in the city squares of imperial Rome. It was a voice which insisted that whatever was being reported was of great significance. It was a rhythm which already told you that there would be no sting in the tale of this story; it was a triumph, otherwise it would not be reported. I found the news bulletins to be the least interesting programmes.

Much more interesting were the many music programmes, in part precisely because there were so many of them but also because they were of very different styles. The most popular group of the moment is the Unhasu Orchestra (one of its former singers is married to the new, young leader, Kim Jong'un). I was told that they sometimes performed at sports stadiums around Korea because the audience demand is so enormous. To me, however, they sound relentlessly bombastic and overbearing; hearing them, I am reminded of Woody Allen's satirical comment on Wagner: 'whenever I hear his music, I feel the urge to invade Poland!' Of an older vintage, but still hugely popular, and certainly more subtle, varied and entertaining, are the groups known as Pochonbo Electronic Ensemble and Wangjaesan (all of these, including Unhasu, can be sampled on YouTube). On this visit, I was shown a concert DVD by Wangjaesan which included one of the most unusual dance routines I have seen. The troupe of about eight male dancers were dressed in enormous hats which covered their bodies down to the knees so that all the audience saw was these nodding hats and the skinny legs. It was obviously a comic dance, the skill of the dancers lying in their ability to jiggle and wobble in harmony. More frequently, the Wangjaesan dancers are lithe women dressed in beautiful, and sometimes skimpy, costumes, performing all kinds of graceful and energetic dances. In between TV programmes, there are often music videos and these usually feature scenes of nature or tell a short story; almost always the story involves a son being separated from, and later reunited with, his mother, a potent mixture of grief and joy (stoicism at the former, floods of tears at the latter) which never seems to reach its use-by date in North Korea or elsewhere in East Asia.

Apart from music, sport, documentaries, and drama serials, a popular genre of programme is the general knowledge quiz. The studio audience for this is usually filled by middle-aged women and the questions revolve around topics such as diet and health. One example I saw had a family answering questions on seafood and nutrition. To be precise, it was the aged father, with his wife silent beside him and his adult children wordless behind, who answered every question with enormous gusto and bullet-proof confidence. The joy for the audience was in watching his mock dismay and disbelief when he was told the correct answer (the barely supressed smile of his wife suggested she had known it all along).

There are some programmes from other countries. A recent Chinese TV serial was very popular in North Korea in large part because it centred on the son of Mao Zedong who died in the defence of the North during the Korean War. In 2010, there was also a major Russian-Korean co-production for the cinema based on events in that war but Russian movies shown on TV usually date from the Soviet-era. I saw various home-grown cartoons (cute animals for smaller children, mountain-based warrior heroes for the older) but I was told that the U.S. programme *Tom & Jerry* was also broadcast (this was one thing I wish I could have seen for myself), albeit to mixed responses. Some older Koreans apparently found *Tom & Jerry* too frenetic and wild.

Having briefly mentioned Chinese TV, this may be the place to add a word about North Korean attitudes towards China. After all, Chinese business and Chinese tourists are the dominant foreign forces in the North. From the schoolchildren, I often heard of a fascination with Chinese history; those who wished to visit China were particularly keen to see places of great historical interest. Little was said about contemporary China. More generally, people in Pyongyang's shops and hotels were obviously familiar with Chinese money and, to some degree, with the Chinese language. I did see, however, on occasion, some frustration with Chinese visitors. Chinese tourists in large groups could, as I occasionally observed, be rather demanding and even arrogant towards the North Koreans. The belief among some Chinese that China is the only thing between North Korea's survival and collapse no doubt has much to do with this. In North Korea, by contrast, it is remembered that Korean-Chinese citizens took refuge in the North during the times of China's greatest internal violence, the Cultural Revolution of the 1960s, and also that China endured a catastrophic famine in the late 1950s to early '60s. It is also remembered that at the very moment when North Korea's politics, economy, and environment were hit by multiple assaults in the early 1990s, China actually added to the country's woes by increasing the prices it charged for food and energy. China also delayed food aid until the peak of North Korea's own famine. For all of these reasons, there are mixed emotions about China in North Korea. Historically, Korea has respected China but the cultural subservience of Korean elites up to the nineteenth century (when the Korean intelligentsia valued Chinese culture over their own) has long since passed, and it may also be that the present-day respect is not supported by very much affection.

For closer inspection of Korean movies, I relied on the various DVDs on sale in the hotel bookshops. These all had Chinese, Russian and English subtitles. I took the advice of my students wherever possible; if they said a movie was interesting, then I was interested in it. Of these, one was called *Pyongyang Nalparam*; it was a story set at the time of the Japanese takeover of Korea and focused on a young practitioner of taekwondo, the Korean martial art. I could see why the boys liked it; it was a story of a youthful hero who fought a giant and brutal oppressor through skill and determination, even at the cost of his own life. Rather more interesting to me, if less so to the boys, was *A Family Basketball Team*. This was more of a comedy about a sport-mad patriarch who insisted that every member of his family must excel at sports. The story revolves around two characters. One is the new daughter-in-law who is much keener on music and reading but who must adapt to early morning family jogs and full-on inter-family basketball matches. The second is a wimp of a son-in-law who only convinced the patriarch to accept him into the fold by claiming to be good at boxing (and who is then shown being knocked out by the punching bag); he is forced to play basketball on the daughters' team, something the daughters regard as a dirty trick by the sons to disadvantage them. The sons reject this, saying that all the women in this family are half-men in any case. The battle of the sexes is the running joke in what is an amiable family comedy.

In one of our informal conversation classes, some of the boys told me that they could see even the latest releases on their computers. Apparently some citizens were following the practice in China and copying movies from their theatre seat (in China, this usually means complete with audience heads and chatter), then posting them on the North Korean intranet. When I asked other groups of boys, however, the general response was that they refused to open such files because they were illegal. Indeed, when I mentioned the practice to Teacher Kim, he was clearly taken aback and exclaimed, 'But that's piracy!' Perhaps it is. However, the government's aim is to use cinema to entertain, educate, or distract its people. The copyists could argue that, in making the films more widely and easily available, and in making no profit for themselves, they are actually assisting in this endeavour; a kind of socialist piracy. I did not hear of any 'pirate' being caught so either they are very clever or the authorities are not unduly concerned about them.

In conversation with some female teachers on an earlier visit, they told me of their wish to visit Sydney because they had seen on TV what sounded like a travelogue, focusing on all the tourist sites and the fine restaurants. I did not have the heart at the time to tell them that the Australian government, in line with the US, bans the entry of all men, women and children from North Korea as punishment for the government's nuclear weapons experiments. So they continue to dream of the day they will be on Manly beach, watching the Pacific roll in, and drinking a chardonnay. In 2011, I was working with people in Australia to change the government's policy in this regard but the administration in Canberra, then and now, was deeply unpopular, deeply divided, and most unlikely to take any decision which might add ammunition to its conservative critics. Far greater hope rested in New Zealand where the government traditionally was more like Canada in taking an independent line in foreign policy. With the support of the New Zealand-DPRK Friendship Society, I started moves to organise a visit by two of my teaching colleagues to schools and universities. It was to be the first visit by people from North Korea to New Zealand for many years.

On this, I had a conversation with my colleague Teacher Kim about images of Korea in the English-speaking world and what any DPRK visitor to New Zealand, or elsewhere, might have to face. It was not a happy talk. I mentioned to him some of the advertising surrounding a recent book by an American journalist called *Nothing to Envy*. This included claims, for example, that secret police would patrol the crowds at mass gatherings and scrutinise the faces of the people; if they were not cheering in the appropriate manner, there would be trouble. Teacher Kim was bemused. If, he suggested, someone wandered through the crowd and suddenly stared at me, I would naturally stare back and so I would obviously be in trouble. Also, if they are supposed to be secret police, shouldn't they do a better job of being inconspicuous? These were obvious responses to what seemed like a ridiculous scenario. Another of the advertising claims, just to show how terrible a place is North Korea, is that the American novel *Gone with the Wind* is banned. Teacher Kim had not heard of the novel (though the textbook excerpts from the work of another American writer, Sinclair Lewis) and so could not say whether this was true or not. He and other teachers, however, did tell me of the American or Western culture which was freely available in the North. Apart from *Tom & Jerry*, there was also American detective fiction (everyone, not just the students, seemed to like detective stories, irrespective of where they came from). Manager Kim had earlier told me that one of his son's favourite films was *King Kong*, and added that they both loved *Mr. Bean* (I enjoyed the irony of contemporary Western culture being represented by a big ape and an imbecile). One day, somewhat mischievously, I took a copy of *The Simpsons* comic book into the class, intending to show the boys what a modern, American comic looked like. I showed this to the teachers in advance to make sure I wasn't breaking too many rules; one of them just said, 'Oh yes, that's the one where the mother has this amazing hairstyle.' So, even *The Simpsons* was not news in Pyongyang.

Money, it's a gas...

One of the topics that most interested my journalist friend, Kōichi, was the question of money, and not just in the hands of children. So, while in Pyongyang, I kept an eye out for any information that might be of use to him. One of the most obvious things is the multinational nature of retailing in the city. The idea that North Korea is reclusive and cut off from the outside world is instantly belied by the myriad currencies used in the shops. In fact, the goods are sometimes priced in Korean *won*, sometimes in US dollars, and sometimes in Chinese *renminbi*, even though the official 'other' currency in the country since 2003, replacing the greenback, is the euro. Every purchase I made in shops large or small, there would always be that moment of consternation as the shop assistant filed through the cash tray and put together a batch of different currencies for my change. Usually, they offered me US dollars, assuming either that I was American, or that like so many Chinese apparently, the US dollar remains the international currency of choice. Normally, I would answer simply that, not being American, I had no use for American dollars and, instead suggest they give me *renminbi* which seemed to be most readily available, certainly much more than euros. One answer to this complicated commerce appeared from 2011 with the start of a new debit card system; you buy the card from one of the issuing banks for whatever amount you wish and then the price of your goods is automatically deducted from the card at the point of sale. To date, I have not bought one of these cards and have only seen them being used very occasionally but I was asked in a couple of shops whether I had one, so they are clearly taking off. I did wonder, however, whether this is but the first step towards that great two-edged sword of the modern system, the beloved and dreaded credit card. So much is changing in North Korea that nothing is entirely unthinkable.

There was another alternative to change where there simply were not the notes or coins available; that was for me to buy more of whatever was on sale until there was no longer any need for change. As my most common purchase was of food or drink, and this took place mostly in coffee shops and restaurants (all apparently well supplied with stock, if not with change), I ended up buying a great deal more than I could ever need. In such places, there also were cigarettes for sale; what seemed to be the three popular Korean brands and sometimes others from Japan, China, Britain or the US. This meant that Teacher Kim, whenever he was with me in this kind of situation, did rather well. I don't recall him ever suggesting I fill out the purchase with cigarettes for him but, if I and the shop assistant were struggling and I asked him to help out, he always graciously accepted a packet (or a carton). If cigarettes were currency, he could probably have opened his own bank by the time I left.

I did suggest to Teacher Kim that life might be easier if I could exchange whatever currencies I had for North Korean money. He agreed in his inimitable fashion, saying 'probably' (which, on this occasion, meant 'let's not talk about it'). I had been told on my first visit in 2006 that foreigners were not allowed to carry *won*. Whatever the reason, I was never, with the one, conspiratorial exception mentioned earlier, offered *won* as part of my change. Then, one lunchtime, as Teacher Kim and I were walking back to the school from the neighbouring restaurant, I saw something glistening in the winter sun on the path. On closer inspection, it turned out to be a silver coin – the smallest denomination, a 1-*won* piece (equivalent to about one-tenth of a US cent) but elaborately decorated on both sides. I picked it up and placed it in my pocket; at last, I had got some Korean money (even if there was nothing I could buy with it)!

There was one aspect of money over which Manager Kim and I did have some difficulty. Late in the trip, he spoke to me over coffee and beer (my coffee, his beer) about one of his grand plans. He had negotiated with the central government and obtained a grant of land near the College. On this, it was his ambition to erect a sports and culture centre for the local children. The only thing missing was the finance. I considered myself a very poor investment prospect but he seemed to think that I might stumble across some business contacts at some point along my travels, and that, with magical eloquence, I could convince them to donate the money for construction. I asked him whether he had spoken to his contacts among the large Korean community in northeast China, the community formed in the 1910s-30s as a refuge from Japanese colonialism. Manager Kim was pessimistic about this source; individuals had contributed generously in the past to education and cultural facilities in the North but these were hard times for many people in China also. He was usually one of the most optimistic and positive people you could meet so it saddened me to see him so disconsolate.

Holiday by Decree

On the second Sunday of my winter 2011 visit, I was due to meet the female teachers Mrs. Kwak and Song plus a group of about ten students at the Art Gallery in central Pyongyang. I had spent several hours there on previous visits and, while I knew the classical paintings to be glorious and the modern ones to be dynamic and interesting, I knew also that the heavy stone building and cavernous gallery rooms were freezing in winter. For that reason, I asked that we meet at 10am, not 9am as originally planned (an hour's delay would probably have made no difference to the temperature inside the Gallery but one can always hope). At about 9.45, I duly appeared in the lobby of Chongnyon Hotel. 'There is a problem,' Teacher Kim told me. 'Large or small?' I asked. He explained: the previous evening, an order had been sent out to government departments, offices and other key points in the community stating that, in order to conserve fuel, no vehicle should be used this Sunday. Manager Kim, apparently, was in his office trying to obtain special permission for us to drive into the city. We were to wait.

I asked Teacher Kim about the alternatives. None seemed feasible (although I doubted this). Perhaps the buses were also off the roads; the subway station was a considerable distance away, etc. etc. We waited. After some time, a call came from Manager Kim; he was still trying to get permission. We waited. Eventually, it became clear that we at least were going nowhere, despite the occasional bus and car that we saw on the main road in front of the hotel. We considered Plan B. Teacher Kim was all for a quiet rest with a good book; I was less thrilled. On the second floor of the hotel, there was a games room with several tables for pool and some for table tennis. We decided to explore.

What I discovered is that Teacher Kim is a mean table tennis player and a very lucky novice at pool! At table tennis, he regularly went for his shots, no holds barred. At pool, on a table where the sidewalls were warped and produced some extraordinary twists of fate, he responded quickly and started to knock the balls in from every angle.

I was insistent that we get out of the hotel at least once that restless Sunday. The first foray did not take us very far. In fact, right next door to the hotel was what we took to calling 'the Chinese McDonalds'. In appearance, from menus to packaging to table tops, it had the look and feel (as well as the taste) of a McDonalds.

Looks familiar? Lunch at one of the 'Chinese McDonald's' in Pyongyang

It was, I was told, a Chinese investment, presumably aimed in part at the many Chinese tourists who stayed at Chongnyon. We had a Sunday lunch of fried chicken and chips with beer in a plastic cup. What can I say? It was what we expected; neither particularly good nor particularly bad. Although we were quite late for lunch, Sunday is a day to take things easy and there were about six or seven other diners in the place, all of them Korean.

On another Sunday, when we were staying at a city centre hotel, Teacher Kim and I, plus Manager Kim, went to an up-market restaurant. We had a private booth, separated not by a wall but by a screen, and the menu was a vast collection of different meat and fish dishes. We all chose a main course, and Manager Kim began to wax lyrical about this place being one of the few where you could still get Asahi Beer, one of the most famous Japanese brands. It had, I was told, been very popular in past years but the deterioration of Korean-Japanese relations in recent years had made it more difficult to obtain (though obviously not impossible). He explained that an Argentinian brewery had begun to export to Korea and that this was now a popular brand. There was also the local Taedonggang Brewery which specialised in beers and cider; I tried the cider and found it very pleasant. The two Kims stuck to beer and vodka to accompany their meals.

As we were talking, an annoying beeping sound kept erupting every few minutes. After half an hour of this, I mentioned it to Teacher Kim and asked him what it was. He shrugged. It happened again. He stood up and peered over into one of the other booths. 'It's some young guys,' he said, 'messing about with their 'phones.' The noise continued and, finally, I said that it was getting on my nerves and that I would go back to the hotel. At that Teacher Kim stood up again, and called out something to the other booth. There was a short reply. 'Ah,' he said, 'these young guys; they just don't care.' The noise continued unabated. At least I learned something else; a teacher is not guaranteed respect by the younger generation in Pyongyang and some of that generation couldn't give a damn about anyone but themselves. On a final note, just as I was leaving (the two Kims having long finished their food), the waitress brought one more dish; she had completely forgotten about it but gave only a perfunctory apology for her mistake. So, I did get a chance to observe noisy youth and sub-standard service all in one place. It really made me long for Chongnyon Hotel.

The Real Achilles Heel of Chongnyon

My usual hotel in west Pyongyang was admirable in many ways, not least for the people who staffed it, especially Migyong, Huiran, Ms. Pak and the others. Its refrigerator-like lobby was a problem in winter but one that I could choose to avoid; the people at the front desk and the gentlemen manning the entrance were less fortunate. The only problem that genuinely grieved me occurred irregularly about 6am; it was the absence of hot water in the shower. A wise man once said, however, that comedy is pain. My suffering with the hotel plumbing did at least give me the opportunity to entertain the boys.

Each day, I rose at 5.45am. Each day, I ventured warily into the bathroom, turned on the hot water tap in the basin, and waited. Some days, I waited more. After about ten minutes, my sense that I was being an eco-terrorist for wasting so much water started to wear me down. I tried the water maybe once, even twice, more; it remained cold. On such days, I had to turn to Plan B. In the room, there was a large hot water jug such as is used all over Asia. It contained about 8-10 cups of water. From this, I would take one cup, empty it into the plastic bowl, and shave both quickly and heedlessly, trying to get it over with before I froze over. Then came stage 2. Stepping into the bath, I half-filled the plastic bowl and, as carefully as possible, poured (or, more accurately, dripped) this over myself. A quick soap-up, then another half-filled bowl for rinse forward, and another one for rinse backward. It was a tricky manoeuvre but I became better at it with practice.

Things became more complicated, however, on one particular morning. On this occasion, the power in my room had been off since mid-evening the night before. I had managed using the battery of my laptop for light from the screen and music to pass the time until about 10pm when I slipped into bed wearing several layers of clothes plus a scarf and hat. This was no great problem and I slept reasonably well. At 5.45 the next morning, however, the power was still off (or was off again) and my laptop was also exhausted. In the darkness, my only recourse was to use the light from the tiny screen of my MP4 player as a torch to guide me to and in the bathroom. No hot water, of course, so now the challenge was to shave in a cup of hot water with one hand while holding the MP4 in the other. My undergraduate students in Australia, all officer cadets in the armed forces and used to roughing it in the bush, would probably see this as simplicity itself. Perhaps it was. Taking a shower in the same manner was something else.

Later, I asked the boys in different classes whether they had enjoyed electricity and hot water that morning. All said they had. I explained my experience to them; it was an opportunity to introduce some different vocabulary to them ('plan B', for example). I also mentioned that the kind women of the hotel had thoughtfully placed a candle in my room for use in a power cut. Unfortunately, they had assumed that I, probably like every other male in the hotel, either smoked or carried a lighter. Thus, there was a candle but no matches. I asked the boys, what should I have done? I gave them a hint as to the imaginative direction I wanted them to go. Several of them picked up on the clue and suggested helpfully that I could have created a spark with stones or two pieces of wood. Ah yes, I replied, but where would I find a stone or pieces of wood on the twentieth floor of the hotel? You would have to climb down the stairs in the dark, they said, and search outside. We calculated the number of steps in total; probably about 500. One of them suggested: you could take the candle with you, then it would be easier to climb back up. Good thinking, I agreed. Another, however, scoffed at the idea that any of this was a real challenge: climbing 500 stairs, he declared, would be good exercise, at any time and in any conditions. No doubt he was right. Thus it was that my misfortune led to a lively discussion.

Surviving Pyongyang Hotel

I had stayed on previous occasions in several of Pyongyang's major hotels, including the towering twin pillared Koryo Hotel in the city centre. I had met some fine people there, especially a great mini bear of a man who was a landscape artist and had a gallery concession on the second floor, and who managed to talk fluently to me for about an hour with less than five words of English but with a great, eloquent vocabulary of body language. I bought one of his landscapes and also, from his collection, an ink study of a group of sea-life by Kim Gi'man, a recently deceased master painter of the Korean art world. The hotel itself, however, was too large and too 'international nowhere' for my taste; in its rooms and lobbies, I could be anywhere. On the present trip, I had asked Manager Kim to find me a different hotel for a few days; my only condition was that it must, simply must, have hot water, morning and night.

His choice was the Pyongyang Hotel, a short walk south from the central rail station, facing Pyongyang's major river, the Taedong. Its attractions included that it was relatively small, just five floors, and had the distinction of being one of Pyongyang's oldest structures. 'Old' in Pyongyang has a clear meaning. As indicated earlier, the US military had absolute control of Korean skies during the war and destroyed anything standing. In fact, Charles Armstrong, a professor at Columbia University in New York, writes that US planes between 1950-53 dropped over 630,000 tons of bombs on the Korean peninsula, almost all of them on North Korea (this was more than 100,000 tons in excess of all the bombs dropped across the whole of the Pacific theatre in WW2). Thus, the modern urban history of the North is one of extremes. In the nineteenth century, it remained the traditional 'land of the exiles', largely unpopulated due to its lack of good farmland. In the colonial 1930s, it went through a shock industrialization and urbanization program conducted by the Japanese overlords. In the early 1950s, all of this was sent back to the stone age. From the later 1950s, entire cities, including of course Pyongyang, were built or rebuilt from scratch. Then, in the twenty-first century, came the time for renovation.

One consequence of this mass reconstruction in 2011-12 was that some students of the College were among the tens of thousands of volunteers contributing time and effort each Sunday on one of the building sites (though I also heard that the professional builders sometimes thanked volunteers for carrying bricks and tile but asked them to help most by just staying out of the way when it came to anything more complicated). Another was that, on my earlier visit, I had experienced what it was like to teach in a semi-warzone. Vast new apartment buildings were being prepared next to the Middle School in the heart of the city and the air was filled with dust. This was in addition to the 'yellow clouds' of sand which flew in from northeast China and which left everyone choking (Manager Kim's solution was to cut the sand with a glass of whisky in the evening – I was unconvinced). A further addition was that every day there would be explosions, the school windows would shake, and my nerves would fray.

We moved from Chongnyon Hotel early on Sunday morning. From behind her thick winter jacket and fur collar, the receptionist at Chongnyon asked me disappointedly why I was leaving – I avoided any reference to the freezing lobby and the interrupted hot water. Instead, I reassured her I would be back in just a few days. To stress the point, I even left behind some luggage (better say garbage – a musical instrument called a pipa I had bought in Beijing and which, despite its mark of 'tested for quality', was broken even before I took it out of its case). Then it was off to Pyongyang Hotel, Manager Kim's promise, on pain of his death, that there would be non-stop hot water very much in my mind. When we arrived, however, it was of course very early and the maid was still preparing the room. She apologised for the delay and began to hurry her cleaning but the fault was all mine so I dropped my case and we headed off immediately for our rendezvous with Teachers Kwak and Song plus another group of about ten boys.

It was after this visit that I began to suspect the Pyongyang Hotel had its own slight problem, at least for me. When I stepped into the room that Sunday afternoon, it was already uncomfortably warm. I looked around for a thermostat but there was none. It was, instead, the traditional *ondol* system of under-floor heating such as was used historically in Korea, China and also in places such as the Roman empire. It was warm! By evening, I had to put on slippers to stop my feet from baking. It was only later that night, however, that I realised just how warm it got. There were two single beds in the room. At about 1am, I awoke absolutely bathed in sweat. The sheets were so damp that I had to move to the other bed. Of course, the same problem happened there; just an hour or so later, I was soaked again. The next morning, I felt exhausted and dehydrated, despite drinking all the water bottles I had carefully accumulated and, when I stepped outside into the cold morning air, my throat was already rasping and I felt like hell. It was not a promising start. I had, however, enjoyed a hot shower.

The next night, the same thing happened. I asked Teacher Kim whether his room was the same. 'It is a bit warm,' he replied with typical understatement. He suggested I fill a bowl with water to put some moisture back in the air; I decided to fill the bath. Still I was melting each night like the wicked witch from The Wizard of Oz. On the third morning, I struggled down to breakfast. It was another of those cavernous dining halls beaming with chandeliers and no windows, while the TV as in other hotels blared out opera – the Unhasu orchestra again - from a DVD. I managed to finish the usual breakfast of yoghurt, omelette and toast, then, in a dream-like state of exhaustion, stagger back to my room. Hardly had I opened the door, however, before my temperature began to rocket and I found myself staring into the basin, vomiting anything and everything there to be found. As the heaving continued, I could imagine Nietzsche triumphantly behind me shouting, 'What does not kill me...' 'Sod off, Freddy!' was my silent response. When everything was over, I looked at my watch. It was 8.05. I was late by just a few minutes. There never really was any question in my mind; I was not going to call in sick and waste a whole day. I wiped my face and went down the stairs. Teacher Kim always asked me if I'd slept well and I always told him the truth. Today, he could see by my white face that things had not gone well so we just jumped into the mini-bus and set off. Arriving at the school, I told him that I would take each lesson as it came; if I couldn't do the job properly, then I would take an hour's rest and reassess the situation. Mrs. Kim came into the room at that point and, hearing of my problems, asked me earnestly to return to the hotel and rest up. I told her that work and her smile were my best medicine and that, if I got through the first lesson, I expected I could do the rest. Throughout that day, she looked after me even more considerately than usual; I don't think I ever had a glass of water or a cup of tea out of my hand, and there was always some snack food to give me sustenance. She also rang the restaurant and asked them to prepare something very light and innocuous for my lunch.

I recalled the comedian's claim that comedy is pain, and I decided to use my plight as material for teaching that day. I told the boys about my response to the *ondol* heating and how it had probably taken a kilo off my weight every evening. They laughed, as I'd hoped they would. I then told them about being ill that morning and how I had imagined Nietzsche behind me. They laughed again. But, I emphasised, I was here and today was my challenge. My only request of them was that they help me out with even more energy and involvement than usual. They all agreed, and that is how I got through that difficult day.

'The warm love of Marshal Kim Jong'il'

It is an accepted fact of the British and other Western media that Kim Jong'il was an 'odious tyrant' (the phrase used by ITV News, London, on the date of his death shortly after I was to leave Pyongyang). The British media luxuriates in happy ignorance about East Asia in general, and about North Korea in particular. One of the most discreditable and degrading examples I recall comes from *The Sunday Telegraph*. It was in an opinion piece by the indefensibly awful celebrity historian Niall Ferguson who never allows truth to get in the way of a good rant and a chance to promote his own name (he has been exposed as a liar by the writer William Dalrymple and denounced as a racist by the Indian scholar Pankaj Mishra). In this, he dismissed Kim Jong'il as a madman largely on account of his appearance; a kind of boiler suit, large glasses and Elvis-style haircut. 'The kind of person', Ferguson insisted, 'whom we would all cross the road to avoid'. Ferguson stated adamantly that Kim had publicly threatened to use nuclear weapons against South Korea if financial aid were not forthcoming. 'Give us the cash or we nuke Seoul!' was his shrill quote. Putting aside the inconvenient fact that the DPRK actually did not have nuclear weapons at that time, the very idea that any Korean leader would threaten mass murder on civilian fellow Koreans is literally unthinkable; it would contradict every Confucian moral principle ever held dear by Koreans individually and as a whole. Indeed, in Ferguson's bizarre little piece we may well ask, between the rabid lie and the racist fantasy of Oriental barbarity, who is the real madman?

Another *idée fixe* of the media is that there are propaganda images of Kim and his father on every street. Having criss-crossed Pyongyang repeatedly over the years, I can only suggest that there is about one billboard, of varying sizes from large to small, for every ten to fifteen blocks. There was a very large billboard just opposite my hotel in west Pyongyang; this was illuminated every night regardless of the power supply elsewhere. But then so was the huge Chinese restaurant just beside it, lit up like a pyromaniac's birthday cake. The image on this billboard was very simple; the two Kims, smiling and seeming to embrace the local residents; no background or text. Its purpose was to serve as a pleasant image, adding colour and warmth to an area filled with tall anonymous apartment buildings, enlivened only by the variety of potted plants that residents placed on their balconies.

In understanding North Korea, some of the dumber ideas need to be ditched or at least questioned. First, North Korea is not a hermit state; that phrase was first used against Korea as a whole in the nineteenth century when Koreans, very similar to the elites of China, showed no interest in the products or practices of Europe and the US. In recent decades, North Korea has enjoyed mutually beneficial relations with two of the most important states of the twenty-first century world: China and Russia. For relatively little cost, China has a major security asset in its northeast region, just an hour's flight from its capital. Russia enjoys a similar benefit on its easternmost land border. With the undeveloped mineral wealth of North Korea, both states are well placed for future benefits. It might also be noted that diplomatic visitors to Pyongyang in the past decade or so have included not only the Russian, Chinese and South Korean presidents but also the prime minister of Japan (the last man to hold that title with any kind of distinction was named Koizumi and, despite being the leader of a centre-right party, he publicly described Kim Jong'il after his meeting as intelligent and witty). Just a few weeks before his death, Kim Jong'il made a visit to Russia's Far East in pursuit of greater trade links. On the shelves of Pyongyang, one can buy goods from a whole host of countries; in 2011, for example, Argentinian brewers had found a new market while, in the electronics shops, you could seemingly buy PCs of any brand you wanted. On the streets, I saw cars from France, Germany, Italy, South Korea, Japan, and even some Fords and Chevrolets. Just because North Korea presently does not have open borders does not mean it is a recluse or a hermit; it is a garrison state technically at war with the most powerful state in the post-1945 world. Yet, as the teachers and school officials had told me, what they desperately wanted was knowledge of the world and, when I brought them copies of the Encyclopaedia Britannica on CD-ROM, they were in such demand that the disks were worn out within just six months.

While outside observers pour scorn on the regime in Pyongyang and insist that citizens obey it only out of fear, the dedication to the system and to the leader of intelligent young men and women is obvious when one actually speaks to them. One of the most common phrases in class or in homework assignments during my time was 'due to the warm love of Marshal Kim Jong'il'. To dismiss this as brainwashing is to miss the point. Were it anything so mechanical, one would hear it from every student and one could predict every situation in which it would be used. Instead, it was used for a variety of situations and by only some of the boys. In other words, each student was making a choice, when and whether to use the phrase. Indeed, the point here is that, where one has choice, one also has freedom. For these teenage pupils, however, among them almost undoubtedly some of the future leaders of the country, it was clear that the general belief was and is that the leader exists solely to oversee their security and welfare; in this, he acts as a traditional Confucian head of state (and, in that sense, the Kim dynasty is easily understood as a familiar form of government in East Asia). Whatever was positive in their lives could be attributed, at least in part, to his benevolence; whatever struggles they collectively encountered, his presence ensured they would be protected. This was no guarantee of success in every venture; no-one was oblivious to the realities and limits of their situation. However, another term I heard again and again was 'striving'. The mood of society, as well as I could judge it, and certainly among its elite youth, was optimistic. Past struggles had not defeated them; if anything, they had tempered society and made it stronger in the face of adversity (Nietzsche would have been pleased). If there was something they presently did not have, for example, open access to the internet, either that would come in the future or they would do without it. They were neither impatient nor dissatisfied. The sales gimmicks of other countries 'buy before it's too late', 'last chance', 'must have', made no sense to them; they smacked only of an enslaved herd-like mentality.

All of this was in stark contrast to political leaders in the countries where I was usually active. French philosopher and social critic Jacques Rancière has written about how leaders in liberal democracies so often present themselves as doctors to an ailing patient. Equally often, the rhetoric of such doctors is of austerity and 'hard measures', 'tough decisions', and 'shared pain' (though clearly the sharing is not equal). All of this weary rhetoric was lampooned mercilessly decades ago in the TV comedy series *Yes, Minister*. Yet it never ends because the clotted lifeblood of our contemporary liberal democracy is political apathy and socio-economic fear. The patient, one might suggest, is alive but comatose.

During my late 2011 visit, Teacher Kim asked me for my opinion on the 'Occupy' protests which, in defiance of the general apathy but certainly sparked by fear, recently had erupted in major cities around the capitalist world. I had brought along a short article on this movement from an English journal. I handed it to him. He read it quickly and said; 'This would be an interesting text for our pupils.' I agreed, and then considered his original question further. Later that day, at lunch in our usual private room, I returned to the issue. I suggested that protest was inevitably going to increase across Europe and probably the US. There was nothing new in this; 1968 is a seminal date in modern history but it is surrounded by peaceful and not so peaceful protests on a score of issues. The expectation of climate change scientists is that there will be catastrophic changes in the twenty-first century to global food supplies. The early warning shots of these catastrophes were evident in the tumult in the Middle East and North Africa in 2011. Changes of government, however, can do nothing to reduce pressure on the world price of such basic foodstuffs as grain. So, I suggested, the immediate future was more than likely to be characterised by intensifying struggles for survival. Within these struggles, a society such as North Korea's, which had already endured and survived the 'hard years' of the 1990s, and which had turned struggle into a collective virtue, might well be even better placed to weather the crises than societies such as Britain, America and Australia, where collective action was the exception, not the norm, and where the individual and his or her rights took clear precedence over one's duty to society. Teacher Kim pondered the idea, both chilling and reassuring simultaneously, and offered no further comment.

The Very Dapper Teacher Ham

I had first met Teacher Ham in unfortunate circumstances on an earlier visit in 2011. He was to take over from Teacher Kim as my translator and guide once I moved from the College to the Middle School in the city centre. It had been arranged that we would meet in the coffee shop of the Koryo Hotel but no particular time had been fixed; 'In the afternoon', I was told. Sunday afternoon grew old and long but no sign of Teacher Ham. By 6 o'clock, I was still waiting and far from pleased. Finally, the call came from Teacher Kim that our visitor had arrived. I went down to see him, with the intention of setting him straight about how things needed to be done if we were to get along over the following week.

He proved to be an utterly disarming man, in his late thirties, dressed in what I learned later was his habitual light suit, waistcoat and tie, round-faced and always with a soft, kindly expression. His voice also was quiet and gentle. It turned out that he had been delayed so long because of his wife. She, it seemed, had long-running health problems and, this day, she had been so unwell that she could not stand without feeling dizzy. Teacher Ham naturally had felt there was no way he could leave her alone. In later talks, he always spoke with deep love and affection for his wife, and she for him. As he explained, his wife often would not eat alone; if he were not there, she would say she had no appetite and go without. No matter how late he might be, she would always wait for his return and then they would share dinner. It was, without doubt, a marriage to admire.

On the present visit, I had originally been scheduled to spend half my time at the College and half at the Middle School. In my first week, however, I was told that there had been a problem at the Middle School; with all of the construction around its vicinity, there had been some damage to the pipes supplying water to the school and the decision had been taken to close it down for an early winter's holiday. So, the children had been told to stay at home and the teachers pursued their own studies. As a result, I only met Teacher Ham socially on a couple of occasions.

Above, two of the compadres. To the left, Teacher Kim, for once out of his usual jacket and tie. To the right, the always dapper Teacher Ham.

Another person whom I was destined to miss on this trip was Mrs. Bak, my Middle School equivalent of Mrs. Kim at the College and an equally charming person. Mrs. Bak was a few years older than Mrs. Kim and had a son already at the Middle School; she told me that she was pleased when she could pick up some terms in English from me because then she had a chance also to teach her son. She was, and is, another elegant woman, always carefully dressed and graceful. As a present on this occasion I had brought for her and Mrs. Kim a selection of French perfumes. In the shops around Pyongyang I had seen perfumes for sale but, in the smaller department stores, these seemed to be largely 'Kylie', 'Beckham' and the like. I did wonder if anyone in Korea had ever seen or heard of Kylie, the Australian pop coquette; the boys never mentioned Beckham (perhaps he was too old for them to admire or simply not skilful enough when compared to Messi). Anyway, I assumed that Guerlain and Givenchy would be more appreciated; even in Pyongyang, people respect the reputation of France for quality goods.

While I was not to see Mrs. Bak (who was away from Pyongyang attending the wedding of a cousin), nor to work with Teacher Ham, he and I did share a quiet dinner (for which I apologised to his wife) and he brought me up to date on various things. For himself, he had spent three weeks recently attending a course on teaching methods run by an international group involving people from Canada, New Zealand, Britain and elsewhere. It had been an intensive affair and there had been a large group of Korean attendees so he had not had much time to spend individually with the foreign teachers. The one thing that he appeared to have taken from it was the importance of visual materials, something about which I have mixed views. The course, however, was another reminder both of the foreign influences on Korean education and, indeed, the desire of Korean teachers to embrace these influences and expand these contacts.

We also spoke about the Occupy protests in various countries and, in England especially, of the hardships for youth, including university students facing increasing fees and declining job opportunities. Indeed, the damage inflicted across society by the so-called global financial crisis made it seem that Britain was headed for the same fate of self-destructive austerity measures as the clutch of European states, including Greece, Portugal, Italy and Ireland. The result would be even more families with no-one working, rising youth alienation, a middle-class in continuing and accelerating economic decline, and growing widespread fear that, even if one could get and hold a job, one's pension would never suffice for retirement. My feeling was that, while the land of England may be green and pleasant, the mood of too many of its people, and for far too long already, was grey and melancholy. Teacher Ham just shook his head and said, 'I am sad to hear all of this. Here, I feel free from such worries. I work and I am rewarded. If I am sick, I will be treated. I do not fear anyone in my community. It seems to me that people in your countries are not free.' This was not said to score a propaganda point. We had spoken long enough and often enough in the past that I could tell it was said seriously and sincerely. It reminded me of the assertion by William Faulkner (with regard to slavery) that you cannot declare someone to be free; genuine freedom is a state of mind and, if a man believes himself to be free, regardless of how he appears to others, then he is free. In order to understand North Korea, it is necessary to acknowledge this reality: that intelligent, informed men and women, not members of the power elite, consider themselves to be free and, looking at our fragmented societies, seeing what is on offer and what is the price to be paid, simply do not envy us.

Being Creative

One of the units in the textbook was on being creative. It began by insisting, 'Everyone is creative. In what way are you?' I used this as a platform for making up stories in class. One day, I asked the boys what they had done on Sunday. Most of the replies were; watch TV, play sport, do homework. Two boys, however, had gone to the Pyongyang Zoo to see the tigers and bears. I jumped on this and roped in their favourite theme – football. What, I asked them, would happen if the two friends became rival trainers of a tigers and bears football team? First, I suggested, we needed a sense of how the players would move. With only the slightest prompting, each of the two boys demonstrated the running style of a tiger and then a bear. But, interjected one of the other boys, how can they kick the ball? We agreed this might be a difficulty. They can use their heads, offered another. Bears can stand, noted one boy. This led to general agreement that bears would have the advantage at spot-kicks. With their love of tigers, however, there were others who insisted that the tigers would win; they would run rings around the ponderous bears. It was a good, lively discussion and Teacher Kim was recording it all on my video camera. If I ever put anything on YouTube, this would be my first choice.

The teachers wanted me to give a test to the classes at the end of my stay so I decided to stick with creativity and ask each pupil to make up a two-minute story in English on 'a day in the life of...' I told them that they could speak about their own lives or, alternatively, about anyone or, indeed, anything. Come the day of the test, virtually no-one chose a day in the life of a schoolboy (or, I noted, that of a soldier). Predictably, there were a few who imagined what it was to be a footballer. One of the most inventive replies, however, was a boy from the far north who described a day in the life not of the footballer but of the football; waiting patiently before the match, being kicked and headed during the game, and then nursing its bruises after. Others went into space and chose to be an astronaut or, in one case, a miner on the moon. Another took the sci-fi approach further and spoke about a day in the life of a time-traveller. In his case, the time travel engine was the TV set; he wormed his way into the box and then set the dial for the future. There, he saw a prosperous Korea and happy Koreans. It was that same optimism I had often witnessed, especially among the young.

Of the one hundred boys who took the test, there was only one case of obvious excess borrowing from the textbook. At my campus in Australia, where the undergraduates are all salaried officer cadets of the military, there are dire warnings everywhere about plagiarism and the punishments to follow but these are treated with amused contempt by a minority and there is open talk of cheating. Usually, the students who are found out insist on their innocence ('I didn't know' is the normal stonewalling defence). The worst example in my experience is of a student on the cusp of graduation who asked his lifelong friend, also in the same class, to lend him his essay so that he could get some pointers. The student then changed the first sentence of each paragraph and submitted the friend's essay as his own. When I showed him the two essays side by side, he pointed to these opening lines and protested, 'some of it is mine!' He also insisted, to my utter disbelief, 'I still have the qualities to be a good officer.' So, with this kind of memory, I was disinclined to be too harsh on a Pyongyang schoolboy who cut and pasted the textbook for about one-quarter of his assignment in a foreign language. Having said that, I did not feel the story should pass and I marked it just below fifty per-cent. Teachers Kim and Kwak were reviewing the marks with me and they agreed that a distinction had to be made between using and misusing the text. Mrs. Kwak said that she would have a quiet word with the boy concerned.

Another way in which we developed creativity was by rethinking familiar objects and looking for new ways to use them. In this, I found a tennis ball was a good place to start. I would hold it up and ask the class, 'Is this a football?' 'No,' they replied. I put it on the floor and kicked it to the back row. 'Is it a football now?' I asked. 'Yes,' came a volley of replies. At this point I interrupted the flow and reminded the class of our rule that no answer be less than three words. 'Yes, it is!' shouted some of the boys. I looked at the boy in the back row who had caught the ball. 'Is it a basketball?' I asked. He looked it, thought for a moment, then bounced it. 'Yes, it is also a basketball,' he declared. I retrieved the ball and then threw it the length of the classroom. Several boys reached out and, to the one who caught it, I gave the task of coming up with a new identity for our ever-changing object. After that, he threw it to another pupil and soon the ball was flying back and forth. After exhausting sports, other creative suggestions from the class included: a projectile with which to smite any invader (we agreed, amid considerable laughter, that this could be the North Korean army's new secret weapon); that one could write a message on it and hurl this to a recipient; if an incision were made in it, it could be used as a container of water; and, building on this, if cut in half, it could serve as two cups on a thirsty day. Suddenly, the ball was no longer a ball; it had melted in the ferment of their imaginations.

A Little Football Hooliganism

Within the first day of meeting any of the boys' classes, I was reminded that they love soccer. I mean, they really love soccer. Given the chance, they would adapt every lesson to the subject of soccer; in one of the textbook units, the subject was sleep and dreams and, when I asked them what kind of dreams they had, the majority said either playing alongside Messi at Barcelona or, more frequently, scoring the winning goal for Korea in the World Cup (preferably against Messi's Argentina). In passing, when I asked them about their nightmares, the answers were entirely familiar to me or anyone; being chased by some threatening creature, or being on the edge of falling from some high place. Such fears clearly are a constant of human life, regardless of social or political system.

Their love of soccer and their adoration of Messi, Ronaldo, and even Pelé who appeared in one of their texts, at least made it easy for me to teach; just add a football theme and I had their instant and undivided attention. I did, however, grow tired of talking about football day after day. Instead, I suggested we arrange a game after classes between two teams of boys led by myself and by one of my most active colleagues, Teacher Cha. This was a great success in that it helped me physically merge with them and remove any kind of distance between us (once the ball was in play, no quarter was given and they pushed and shoved me and Teacher Cha just as hard as we pushed and shoved them). Teacher Cha also clearly loved to play any kind of sport with his boys; the only drawback for him, perhaps, was that my team always seemed to win. So, we built up an ongoing, but healthy, rivalry.

Teachers Kim and Kwak often watched these matches from the sidelines, Teacher Kim keeping a water bottle handy for me in times of greatest need, Teacher Kwak nominally being the timekeeper. I say nominally because every time I asked her how long there was to play, she habitually said two minutes. I am sure that some of our games were the longest on record. At the end of the first match, and having played a suspiciously long time, I admitted to Teacher Kim that I was shattered and that, for the last ten minutes I had been holding back and holding back. Teacher Kim smiled and said, 'There is a proverb in Korean: the old cow knows the short road home.' At least he didn't tell me this time, as he so often did, 'you are not young anymore'!

Being winter, the temperature could plummet overnight in Pyongyang. Some days, it was too warm for December (I thought again of the unfermented kimchi and all the disappointed diners); others, it fell to minus nine overnight and stiff, chill winds whipped around the school grounds in the afternoon. After playing one game outside (another victory to my team, I'm afraid), I suggested we play our next one in the school gym. As the temperature dropped outside, the inside became much more attractive. When we came to play the second game, however, Teacher Cha was absent (I was told he had strained his back) and so Teacher Kim valiantly took his place. In fact, Teacher Kim played well and hard, something the boys certainly understood. In this game also, no quarter was ever given and the smaller boys especially used to throw themselves into tackles, and stick to the task like a dog with a bone until they were beaten or, just as often, scrambled the ball safely away.

While we were playing (my hamstrings torn in the first minute as usual), I noticed someone emerge at the entrance to the gym, take one look around, and then start shouting something before disappearing in a huff. I thought nothing about it at the time but there were to be ramifications later.

It was the following week. I had just finished my first informal class with female students and was feeling upbeat; it had gone far better than I had been led to believe. As the girls were filing out, I began to get ready for the indoor soccer match we were to have in the next few minutes. At that point, Teacher Kim said, 'There is a problem.' By this time, my habitual reply to this statement was, 'This is Pyongyang; there is always a problem,' which was over-harsh but was, in part, my attempt to make light of his worries. On this occasion, the problem was the angry young man last seen at the gym. It turned out that he was in charge of the gym and resented it being used for this dangerous game of soccer. In fact, he refused to allow 'his' gym to be used again for indoor soccer on the grounds that the ball was being kicked so high, it could easily damage the roof. In his view, I was told, we had two choices; play soccer outside or play basketball inside.

Conflict is naturally interesting. When passions are high, people can reveal a very different side to themselves and, in that sense, I welcome a dispute and usually observe it dispassionately. This, I thought, was an opportunity to see how disputes in Pyongyang could either develop or be resolved. My first response was to heighten the stakes because I had been left in the dark about events until the very last minute. So I put a challenge to Teacher Kim, and to Manager Kim who had the misfortune to walk through the door at that precise moment: 'If this man wishes to criticise my actions, I expect him to do so in person. I will wait here and he can tell me face to face that I am forbidden by him from using the school's gym.' I sat down again. Teacher Kim asked me to forget about it; we could reschedule the game for another day when the weather outside was better. I repeated that I would remain in the meeting room until the master of the gym appeared. Then I was told he was unavailable; he had already gone home. I thought the man had already lost his argument precisely because he had publicly lost his temper, and because he had proclaimed this blanket ban without any hint of courtesy or conciliation. So I then undermined his position, suggesting to the two Kims that a 'real man' would not act in such a manner, and that the idea of a football defying gravity so deftly as to reach the high gym ceiling was beyond the laws of physics. I managed to get their agreement that the situation was, at the very least, verging on the ridiculous and that they would speak to the offended gym keeper. With that, we left for the hotel and another of our after-work conferences at the refrigerated coffee shop, Teacher Kim smoking more than usual, and Manager Kim commenting on the beer while also looking wistfully at the pack of cigarettes on the table and saying, 'I have given up. My wife is very happy. I will just try one...'

It was, I think, the following lunchtime. As usual, Teacher Kim and I were dining by ourselves in the private room of the restaurant just outside the school gates. The tall, gentle and cheerful waitress who always served us, brought in the first of the several courses, smiled and left. Then Teacher Kim leaned over and said, 'You can use the gym. The principal, Professor Oh, intervened and said, Stewart works for us, he works very hard and he works for free. The least we can do is lend him our facilities when he requests them. So, there is no problem.' 'There is no problem,' I repeated. 'Are you sure? Remember, this is Pyongyang'. Teacher Kim just smiled and said, 'Probably.'

I thought it was time to be conciliatory so when we turned up for the game that afternoon (Teacher Kim on the sidelines again, using my video camera to record part of the action), I told the boys we would play to a new rule; any ball deliberately kicked or thrown above head height would result in a penalty. This would be taken from the centre of the pitch, the opposing goalkeeper removed, and the goalposts (two jackets on the floor) reduced to a gap of about one and a half metres. In practice, this made the game much better; it encouraged more of a passing game (the term is relative as dribbling, head down and hell bent on glory, remained their tactic of first choice) and it gave regular scoring opportunities to each team. It also protected the gym ceiling so I would like to think that the thesis of the gym keeper, modified by my antithesis, resulted in a very satisfactory synthesis. Certainly I never saw the gym keeper again or witnessed any other kind of outburst.

'Have you heard the one about...' – Korean Jokes

I have always believed that humour is one of the most important parts of human interaction and, thus, one of the most important things to study when trying to understand another society. It is also a vital defence against adversity, whether in war or any other form of crisis. One of the principal reasons I had become fascinated with Korea on my first visit in 2006 was the range and quality of humour I had heard from my tour guides. In teaching, I wanted to see if the boys could handle humour in a foreign language; it was certainly a challenge. Little did I know what I was about to unleash.

In the first week of classes, I explained to the boys about my views on humour and its cultural value. I then told them that their homework for the evening was to search their joke books and write out a joke first in Korean and then translate it to English. So, if their parents heard their sons laughing and scolded them for any reason, I reassured them, they could legitimately say they were engaged in serious study. I also gave them an example of a joke that I heard from a schoolboy on my previous visit. It goes like this.

A North Korean soldier is on the frontline when shooting breaks out. He decides to run home and nips off smartly while the bullets continue to fly all around him. Arriving at his village, a local army officer sees him and can't believe his eyes. 'What are you doing?' the officer demands. 'You are a Korean soldier; a Korean soldier does not run away from battle. He stands and fights!' The soldier stands to attention and answers firmly: 'Sir, I am a Korean soldier and I am not running away from battle.' The officer looks unconvinced and demands an explanation. 'Well, sir,' begins the soldier, 'it's like this, see. The shape of the earth is rounded like a tomato. All I am doing is attacking the long way round!'

As I got to the punchline of this joke, all the boys in the class joined in. They had, they told me, heard it a million times before. But it was still a good joke in anybody's language. I told them I would look forward to hearing their jokes in the coming days. No wonder I was impatient every morning to get to school.

Over the following days, I called on five to six boys towards the end of each lesson to stand up and tell us their joke as a way of bringing the class to a happy close. The jokes were of varying subjects and varying quality but they were never in short supply and they all told me something. One of the recurring themes was about 'capitalist society'. This wasn't necessarily negative or critical; it was just a device for distancing the joke from their own surroundings. Here are some examples from the classroom of life and humour as they appeared in 'capitalist societies'.

A man who liked to drink and often drank too much used his mobile 'phone to call a local bar. He asked the barkeeper, 'what time do you open the doors?' The barkeeper replied, 'We open at 11am.', then put the 'phone down and went back to his chores. A moment later, the 'phone rang again and it was the same caller with the same question. The barkeeper was already irritated and gave the same answer before banging the 'phone down. Seconds later, the 'phone rang for a third time, the same caller asking the same question. 'Look,' the barkeeper said angrily, 'I've told you already. We open at 11am. You can't get in even one second before!' The caller shouted back, 'I don't want to get in; I want to get out!'

A new commercial building opened with three stores all selling the same thing. To attract customers, the shop on the left wing put up a huge sign, 'Best stock in town!' To counter this, the shop on the right-wing put up its own sign, 'Best prices in town!' Afraid of losing his business, the shopkeeper in the middle worried all night about what to do. Finally, he hit upon a solution. The next morning, he put up his own sign – 'Entrance'.

Another theme was to use the sanity of insanity for comic effect. For example, a doctor in an asylum conducted an experiment. He drew an imaginary door on the wall of the patients' common room. As he expected, the patients, noticing the door, grabbed the imaginary handle and struggled to get out. He took notes. While doing so, he remarked that one patient alone was sitting quietly in a chair, observing the mob with a satisfied smile. The doctor approached and asked, 'Why aren't you joining the rest in trying to go out?' The sitting patient laughed, 'Those people are just plain mad if they think they can get out there,' he said. 'Oh,' said the doctor, intrigued. 'What's your reasoning?' 'Well,' said the patient, 'because I've got the key!'

Virtually no target was off-limits. Above I related the well-known joke about desertion in the army. The authority of school principals (and of army officers) was also fair game. Thus, one joke begins: a boy turned up to school on the day of a test. The principal saw that he had no pencil and asked fiercely, 'Boy, where is your pencil?' 'I did not bring it, sir', replies the boy. 'What!! No pencil! Don't you know, boy, that turning up for a test without a pencil is like a soldier turning up for battle without his rifle. Have you, boy, ever heard of a soldier turning up for battle without a rifle?' he demands. The boy thinks for a moment and then smiles: 'Yes sir, I have.' The principal is outraged and shouts, 'What's this? You have heard of a soldier turning up for battle without a rifle! What kind of soldier, boy, would do such a thing?' 'Well, sir', replies the boy, 'a general!'

Earlier, I mentioned some risqué stories I heard on my first visit. To round out this section on jokes, I add one example of adult humour that I heard at that time. In summer, a young woman is swimming off the popular beach at Wonsan. Suddenly, the tide shifts and she finds that her trunks have disappeared. In consternation, she wonders how she can emerge onto the crowded sands. Then she spots a placard mounted in the water's edge. Twisting this loose, and holding it across her hips, she rises from the sea. As she does so, the sunbathers all begin to laugh. She is confused until she looks down and reads the sign – 'Warning. Danger zone. Entry reserved for strong men!'

Female Pupils (at last!)

From my earliest visit as a teacher, I had asked to be given a class of female pupils. At the two schools where I worked, classes were separated by sex. Teaching one hundred boys and zero girls, however, seemed to me highly unfair. At that time, I discussed the prospect with Teacher Kim. He said he would see what could be arranged at the College but he warned me that the female pupils were far inferior in English-language ability and so I should not expect to conduct anything like the free-flowing classes I enjoyed with the boys. Undeterred, I continued to argue that we should at least see for ourselves and not dismiss the girl students without a trial. At that time, and again on my second visit, nothing happened. The girls, I was told, were all terribly busy with preparations for this or that cultural event. Before arriving in November 2011, I made it clear by email that, on this trip, I was to teach some girls or else….

Initially, I was given the same old line: the girls weren't good enough, it would be a waste of my time, and they were all busy every day in long-term practice for the following April's celebrations of the 100th anniversary of Kim Ilsung's birth. I got the message, but I also chose to ignore it. It seemed to me that the best way to get anything done was simply to continue pressing the logic of one's position and make light of the obstacles. Finally, after several days of this, Teacher Kim told me one morning, without any great fanfare, that I would be meeting a select group of female pupils that same afternoon.

Our meeting took place in the large visitors room I often used for informal classes. At 3.15pm, Teacher Kim and I were resting after the boys' class which had just finished. Mrs. Kim offered me a cup of coffee and a smile of encouragement. I think she was quietly pleased that the girls were to be given a chance to prove themselves. At that moment, Teacher Kim went to the door to see if they were coming; they were all waiting outside along with their teacher, the always jovial Mrs. Han who regularly mocked herself as overweight. In they filed, all nervously looking around, some carrying in chairs, all except one young lady who made immediately for the chair beside mine and took possession of it against all rivals. I was to learn that she was Ms. Soh, acknowledged as one of the sharpest and brightest students in the College, male or female. She was also very nice-looking with a sweet, perfectly round face, a toothsome smile, and a very gentle, painfully polite, way of speaking, but her will and determination were made of iron. Sitting on my other side was a tall young woman, Ms. Ham, probably 5' 7'' in low heels, with an athletic build that suggested she would be good at volleyball, and a slightly squared but pleasant face with eyes brimming with lively interest and endless good humour. These two obviously could not wait to start and I knew immediately that, despite all of Teacher Kim's warnings, the afternoon would be alright.

The way I usually started a conversation with pupils was by asking what, I thought at least, were simple questions about themselves. So, I told the girls that I believed they were studying various subjects including music and dance. 'No', they replied in unison, somewhat mystified. 'So you don't study music and dance?' I asked, trying to make sure of the basics before we went any further. It turned out that they did study music but not dance; that was the reason for their negative response. I asked them what instruments they studied; there was a wide range of answers including piano, guitar, violin and trumpet. At that moment, Teacher Han interrupted. She was sure that some of her girls had learned to dance. She questioned them quickly in Korean. I wanted to keep the group away from Korean and focused on English so, as soon as there was a moment's pause, I switched tactics and asked her if <u>she</u> knew how to dance. 'Yes, of course!' she replied 'but I am too fat and not a good dancer. You don't want to see me dance!' I assured her that, on the contrary, I would be very pleased to be her audience right then and there. I asked the girls if they had ever seen their teacher dance and they all replied, no. So, it was decided. 'Well,' she concluded, 'if I am to perform, I will need a partner.' She spoke again in Korean and Ms. Ham, as tall as her teacher but slimmer and so mirroring her nicely, stood up. Side by side, and with arms on each other's shoulders, they moved easily into a few steps left, then right, similar in a way to the dance of Anthony Quinn and Alan Bates in *Zorba the Greek*. The other girls clapped in rhythm as the two women, one very young, one of more mature years but perpetually young at heart, smiled and swayed to the beat.

The first meeting with female pupils ended with a series of photos. Ms. Ham is on the left of the photo here.

The one thing the girls really wanted to know about was the life of children their age in Australia. They asked me; what hours did they spend at school, what subjects did they study, what did they want to be later in life, what did they do outside of school, did they, like themselves, have Children's Palaces devoted to their cultural interests? I did not have the heart on this first meeting to tell them my impressions; that teenagers in Australian schools seem to endure their time either bored, frustrated or frightened. That the one place where they seem to feel at home, (certainly not at the family home, yet another place of boredom and frustration), walking endlessly around, slurping goo from styrofoam cups and gazing vacantly on 'stuff' they can't afford, is in the four walls of the shopping malls. As for Children's Palaces, well, if only...

As for themselves, they told me that their own days were indeed heavily occupied with study, music or other practice, and homework. The one day of partial rest was Sunday when, like the boys, they would spend a good part of the day watching TV (they seemed not to share the boys' interest in computer games). Their ambitions also mirrored the boys in that most of them hoped for a career in computer science. Ms. Ham was alone in wishing to become a teacher of English; Ms. Soh, I heard later, was being groomed as a TV announcer.

After the girls had left, Teacher Kim asked me for my thoughts. 'You saw them,' I replied. 'For a first meeting with a native speaker, they relaxed quickly and, if nothing else, they now know for a fact that they can communicate in English. Problems and confusion arose sometimes, but nothing insurmountable. As for being far below the skill level of the boys, there were pupils here today who are a match for nearly any boy I have taught.' Teacher Kim, supportive as usual, agreed and said that he too had been impressed by them.

Before the second meeting with the girl pupils, I tested an idea on Teacher Kim. The previous day we had discovered the dancing talents of Teacher Han, and the night before I had seen a comic dance performed by the group Wangjaesan. Today, I thought it was my turn. Not being blessed with the ballroom skill of a Tosh Twinkletoes (the wonderful *nom de guerre* of a Japanese-born salsa expert near my home town in England), I had decided to borrow a classic routine from Chaplin. Our discussion got off to an excellent start when Teacher Kim told me that the girls undoubtedly knew of Chaplin; there had been a very popular documentary on him on Korean TV (he was right – when the girls later arrived, they instantly recognised his name). That left us with the question of the routine: it was the bread roll dance from *The Gold Rush* where Chaplin, in a dream sequence, performs for a group of lady visitors by putting forks into two small, rotund bread rolls, and twirling them on the table as if they were his tiny feet. It worked better of course for Chaplin; his natural dexterity, plus the exquisite facial expressions he could conjure (aided beautifully by his agile moustache), all made for a magical scene. Putting aside my lack of Chaplin's talent and my blander looks, my major problem was in finding the right kind of bread. There was a tray of freshly-baked rolls in the hotel cafe every morning and I had picked up some of these but, on closer inspection, they were too soft to retain the toothpicks which were all I had to spear them. Mrs. Kim observed my plight and began hunting for alternatives. In the end, we had to settle for a couple of digestive biscuits. The girls were intrigued by this new form of dancing and laughed politely but the thin disc of the biscuits was wrong and it really wasn't Chaplin.

Continuing with the use of music, I mentioned to them that I had brought some songs on a netbook that I was going to donate to a school in the provinces through Manager Kim. They were curious to know what kind of music I listened to. Mostly what I had with me was John Mellencamp and the Irish folk singer Christy Moore, each in his way a kind of Woody Guthrie in that the songs were mainly about the lives, the troubles, and the small pleasures of ordinary people, and more than anything about compassion. I would liked to have played Mellencamp's 'Human Wheel' for them, one of my favourite songs, but the lyrics and the delivery were maybe too difficult for first-time listeners in a foreign language. Instead, I opted for Christy Moore's version of 'Ride On', a hypnotic song of love and loss with a quite simple chorus; it also fit in broadly with the textbook used by the boys and girls with its lesson on the revival of Irish culture after independence from Britain and especially the importance of music. So, Christy, if you ever read this, know that there was a group of girls in Pyongyang who, one afternoon in December 2011, listened transfixed to every word of your song – fair play, man!

On our last day together, I began by giving the girls some small mementos; a colourful pen and a notebook in which I inscribed good wishes to each of them. I then ran through a series of things that I wanted to show them, including a piece of aboriginal art (one of their texts included information on the Aboriginal peoples of Australia). To do this, I asked them to gather round me as I laid these things on the long, low table. Once again, I noticed how comfortable they were with physical closeness; as we all sat on the floor, we were a tight group, shoulder to shoulder, and, unlike my experiences in Japan, no-one seemed in the slightest degree nervous about being so near a foreign adult male. I was their teacher; a teacher is their protector; *ipso facto*, there is nothing to fear from one's protector.

When the College had originally been hesitant about letting me teach girls, I had wondered whether this was a kind of discrimination, common across East Asia (and not so long past in Europe), that boys always come first. So, I had pressed Teacher Kim, always the man in the middle and taking hits from all sides, saying that I could not believe a socialist society would discriminate against its women. I can't say whether that argument had any effect. However, it did prompt a memory of an article I had read in the *Korea Times* from Seoul in 2009. The topic was the rights of women in the North and the journalist, interviewing a former citizen of the North, cited as her key example the difficulties faced by women who chose to cycle. It seems, the article explained, that such women would be regarded as behaving immodestly. It reminded me of how female cyclists in Japan a century earlier faced abuse (and even children throwing stones at them) for being so unconventional and even 'alien' in their actions and attitudes. In Pyongyang, I did hear that only small girl children were generally acceptable on bicycles. This 'prohibition' surprised me slightly in that I have seen a film from Iran, much more conservative of course in its dress codes for women, in which there is a scene of a large group of women engaged in a long cycling sequence.

More broadly, it seemed that women in North Korea have certain advantages. To protect and enhance the rights of women in society was one of the major features of government thinking in North Korea from its very first days; in 1946, there was the Gender Equality Act which gave Korean women the right to equal education and pay, to make their own choices over marriage and divorce, and the right to vote and stand for election to office (regrettably, just as there has yet to be a female leader of China or Japan, it seems unlikely we shall see a female head of the DPRK for some time). In 2001, the government also signed the UN Convention on the Elimination of All Forms of Discrimination Against Women. One can, of course, dismiss all of this as just for show but, among all the foreign criticisms made of the North, I have never heard any suggestion of parents aborting a female foetus, or abandoning a girl at birth because the male is the key provider for their old age. Yet, in China, this has been a cause of outrage both historically and in the present; a state campaign from Beijing in 2011, for example, continued to insist 'Mistreatment and abandonment of baby girls is strictly prohibited'. In India also, the problem of female infanticide is said to be widespread; in my teaching on India, I use a film called *Matrubhoomi: A Nation Without Women* which is an impassioned plea for an end to violence towards girl babies. In present-day North Korea, women are said to be the major contributors in the informal economy where, by making things or growing foods, they bring in much of the household income. The images of women in North Korean film are often a mixture of toughness and tenderness – both are equally on display in the 2006 film *A Schoolgirl's Diary*, the first North Korean film shown at the Cannes film festival. The same is true of the comedy *A Family Basketball Team*. As for the women I observed directly, Migyong was the gentlest and the shyest but she did not hesitate to approach me, despite all the hurdles of language. Other waitresses in restaurants and coffee shops appeared perfectly capable of dealing with any male customer. The same was true of tiny Huiran, the masseuse, and certainly of the female tailor (even Manager Kim had been cowed into near silence in her presence). The women teachers were, with the exception of the youngest just starting out, all strong, independent personalities. If they encountered what they believed to be discrimination or any kind of abuse based on their sex, I have no doubt they would speak out, and do so forcefully.

Finishing Up

It is Thursday evening. I have one more day to teach on this trip. Now I am in my hotel room, listening as usual to a few songs from the netbook in the background, and looking back on what I have seen and done. The netbook itself is a reminder; for three weeks, I have not used the internet or email and it has been just so very good to be away from all of that. No Yahoo with its endless depiction of the world and humanity as freak show (as I review these lines in 2013, today's Yahoo news headline is 'Teacher lets kids taste her blood' - and people describe North Korea as bizarre!). No flashing, flickering adverts (Lonely hearts! Lose weight! Make money!) on every screen; no avalanche of spam from people declaring me the beneficiary of a vast legacy, offering to make me a sexual amazon, or telling me that my bank account has a problem in need of immediate redress – 'just send us your details and you too can have peace of mind'. No salacious gossip about those who populate the human media zoo: just peace and quiet to work, to think, to rest. Even walking in the street, there is a different mood. There is no bombardment of adverts; think of being liberated from that daily assault on your senses. No shopwindows with that now meaningless word 'sale' crying out for your attention (or maybe the word is not meaningless – instead it now has the literal meaning just of 'things for sale'). Streets, in contrast to those of London or Sydney, in which people rarely are seen hurrying or seem overtly harried. Schoolchildren, some of whom, think and talk like young adults; adults who generally are kind and courteous. I have no wish to paint a romanticised view of Pyongyang; I am still dealing with power cuts and cold showers but these seem trivial things when compared to the positives I see around me. I know I will leave this city and these people in just over twenty-four hours, and it is time that I did (my energy is spent and my muscles are torn). However, I know also that I will be sad to leave and I will immediately begin to plan my next visit.

On past occasions, I had been farewelled at the College courtyard by two ranks of all the one hundred boys I had taught plus a group of teachers. As I shook hands with each boy, the clapping continued. In the harsh chill of a December afternoon, I thought this was too much for them to bear (even if, as I had been told, young boys feel no cold) and, in advance, asked this time for a low-key departure. Thus, on the last day of teaching and in the final few minutes of each class, I reminded them that I had to leave Pyongyang the next day but that I would return and see them the following May. I then went round the class, shaking the hand of each boy and exchanging a few words. As I did so, I noticed a difference: when I had first met them and shook their hands, the majority of pupils had looked nervously at the floor to avoid my gaze (in contrast to the female pupils); now, they were relaxed and looked straight at me.

One hurdle I had deliberately chosen to avoid was a last-night banquet. In fact, I tried various stratagems to avoid any kind of banquet at any time. I was continually being told that Korean courtesy demanded the serving of seemingly endless courses of different meats, fishes and seafood, plus vegetables, pickles, fruits, noodles and rice, as well as glasses of differing alcohols to any unsuspecting guest. Well, by now, I was a deeply suspecting guest and had learned my lesson. So, I had worked out my reasoning against an evening banquet (I would not be able to finish the 'homework' the College had given me, that is, the checking of their new draft textbook). As an alternative, I had suggested a farewell lunch with Professor Oh, the principal, and some others. I assumed the pressure of work and time would mean this was a short, simple affair. In relative terms, that proved to be true but only in relative terms.

Immediately after finishing the fourth class of the morning, we drove off to the city centre. There was Manager Kim, Teacher Kim, and Mrs. Kim. Our destination was the restaurants beside the Ragwon Department Store. As we arrived, the power was off and, abandoning the lift, we walked up the stairs. As we did so, the power resumed. We were shown into one of the private dining rooms; waiting there was Professor Oh, Mr. Bak, the department head, and one or two other officials of the school. Our driver shortly joined us. Professor Oh began proceedings with a short but generous speech in which he thanked me for working relentlessly over repeated visits on behalf of the school, its pupils and teachers. We would meet again later that day, he said, but now there was a very special present he wished to bestow on me. Teacher Kim and Manager Kim were looking on in approval; they obviously were in the know. Professor Oh took out a small box and opened it; it was the official school badge, given only to members of the College. With a mischievous smile, he asked me: 'Do you want me to pin it on or do you want Mrs. Kim to perform the honours?' I answered with careful diplomacy that I was proud simply to be a recipient. Showing that he and I were genuinely like-minded, he nodded in understanding and gestured for Mrs. Kim to take the badge. With that most enchanting smile, she carefully pinned the badge to my lapel and then held my hands, still beaming. As the others clapped, the food began to appear. An hour later, it was still coming.

Saturday morning, 7am. It is grey and chill in Pyongyang. In a few hours, I am to speak to an audience of foreign correspondents in Beijing. I am not thinking of that just now. I am cold-showered and packed. I take the slow elevator down to the lobby. Manager Kim and Teacher Kim are both there already, settling their bill. I leave my case with them and say I will return at our agreed time: 7.15. I then run up the stairs to the mezzanine and into Dining Room 4. Migyong is there, alone and waiting. She bestows on me that smile of welcome I treasure. I sit down and she brings me a cup of insam-ch'a, ginseng tea. There is no time for breakfast. The night before, she had offered to get up early so that some food could be readied; the hotel did this for any guest who had to leave before the normal time. I thanked her but refused. I wanted her, I explained, to sleep long and well. With the clock ticking, there was not much to say. I asked her what she would do on Sunday with her husband; 'See a movie,' she replied, 'there are so many to choose from.' It was a comforting thought that this enchanting woman was now embarking on a new adventure, complete with husband and, shortly, a child. I had prepared a letter for her in my 'survival Korean'. It really just said 'thank you' for all the kindness she had shown me on so many occasions. I also explained that I could never have done my job without her encouragement, especially when I was fighting colds and 'flu along the way. Unable even to finish the tea, I left the letter on the table for her to read later. We then walked to the great wooden doors of the dining room. Before opening them once again to the outside world, I put my arms around her, held her close, and uttered just the simple Korean phrase 'annyonghi gessoyo!' It translates as 'goodbye' but its literal meaning is 'be in peace'. As I walked down the stairs, collected my case, and headed out to the car, she was still standing and waving. I waved back and then I was gone.

In the car en route to the airport, Manager Kim spoke about the next visit. 2012 was a big year for Korea and there would be many foreign visitors to this supposed 'hermit nation'. He wanted again to check my dates so that he could be sure of booking a room. At the airport, as I was about to go through the security gates and leave them behind, he said to me in a sombre tone; 'We don't want you to go.' There were times when I was not sure if he were being serious or setting up a joke. Having had enough sadness with Migyong, I decided to choose levity on this occasion. 'Is that right?' I asked. 'So where did you put the drugs?' Without missing a beat, he replied: 'In the suitcase. The guards have been warned. See you in a minute.' Then he laughed, with that great, unreserved laugh, that laugh I associated with Russians and Cossacks, and, of course, some Koreans, especially those who loved life, and women, and laughter.

I am in Beijing. The foreign correspondents and other interested parties have taken their seats. The fire behind me is turning me into toast. Kōichi is calling the gathering to order. He mentions something about the other books I have written: I think to myself, they are all in the past; they don't count. I am impatient to start the talk; usually, once I start, the adrenalin kicks in and everything begins to make sense. I open with an assertion designed to capture their attention. It is, 'This morning I left Pyongyang and I cannot wait to go back; it is where, as a teacher, I have more fun than any place on earth...'

A Report from Pyongyang, December 2011

A few days after I left Pyongyang and returned home to England for Christmas, there was an announcement that Kim Jong'il had died. In view of the turgid stereotypes being dusted off and re-broadcast by the Western media, a long-time academic analyst of the North in New Zealand, Dr. Tim Beal, asked me for a short piece to post on his authoritative website. Though it repeats some of the points made earlier in this work, I add it here as it summarised some of my reflections and experiences at that particular time. It reads as follows.

Until 10 December 2011, I was spending another three weeks teaching one hundred boys and ten girls aged fourteen at one of Pyongyang's leading middle schools. My job was to assist them in practicing and familiarising themselves with communication in English. Put simply, this involved reading and discussing the essays in their English-language textbook, engaging them in classroom conversation on a wide range of topics, and, in informal group chats, finding out more about them, their lives and their ideas.

I left Pyongyang on the morning of 10 December and, in the afternoon, gave a presentation in Beijing to the Foreign Correspondents Club of China on what I had seen and heard. Many of the questions were thoughtful, seeking only better to understand. However, one European journalist asked, 'What is the impact of the famine?' I could only reply, 'Which famine? The only famine as such in Korea was in the 1990s.' He was unconvinced. Later, he popped up again and, not asking but insisting, declared 'There is no industry in North Korea!' I had earlier told the journalists about the visible increase in the number of cars on Pyongyang's roads in just the six-month interval since my last visit. I had also mentioned that many of these new cars were made in North Korea (the company uses Fiat technology and, having ridden in one of them, I can say it is no different to being in any mainstream modern sedan). The gainsayer was unconvinced again.

I regularly encounter this attitude when I speak to people about North Korea. It seems I or they are living in a science-fiction world, an alternative universe in which nothing is, or can be, as it seems. In a book from 2005, *North Korea: The Paranoid Peninsula – A Modern History*, the author, who is trying to get to the truth but is heavily, and disastrously, reliant on the words of defectors and refugees, describes a 'normal day in the life of Pyongyang'. In this, he explains that shopping is a desperate activity because the shelves are so swiftly emptied (I never saw an empty shelf in any of the large or small shops I entered), people struggle to obtain socks or underwear (I cannot comment on the latter but everyone I saw at work or in the street was warmly, and some elegantly, dressed), while personal 'phone ownership is rare and virtually every call is monitored. This last is, after all, only what one would expect of 'the most repressive society on earth' (the stock phrase on amazon.com from anyone commenting on works about North Korea). But in my universe in 2011, the streets of Pyongyang are awash with people using mobile 'phones with complete abandon. In a hotel coffee shop, the waitress wanted to explain the name of a dish to me in English; she could not find it on her in-phone dictionary so she 'phoned a friend in the hotel dining room. If the security services were listening in, maybe they did learn something (the English word 'noodles'). Go to a cafe or restaurant and mobile 'phones are ringing all over the place. Even schoolchildren have mobile 'phones (the younger ones do not bring them to school but the older girls do and use them openly in the school grounds).

Elsewhere, there is an article from 2006 by Dr. Andrei Lankov, an old friend and colleague and also one of the leading commentators on North Korea. In this scholarly piece, he explains about the natural death of what he calls 'North Korean Stalinism'. The definition of Stalinism that he offers begins with 'a system of mass terror' and ends with 'a system of personal dictatorship'. The only problem is that, nowhere in his essay, does he identify anything corresponding to a system of mass terror in North Korea and, without terror, our understanding of the term 'dictator' or 'dictatorship' must radically change. Indeed, one of the principal differences as far as I am concerned between Korea and China is that, in Korea, there has never been anything remotely approaching the regime-sponsored internal brutality of the Cultural Revolution (about which I have heard at length from my wife's family who were among its countless victims). So let me state this here and now: in all of my visits to North Korea over the past two years, I have seen not a single instance of personal or collective terror or even fear (with one exception – when a young woman was about to enter the hotel lift and saw it empty but for me – she froze in fear or consternation and, as the lift doors closed, for once I forgot that I pride myself on being a gentleman and did not try to reopen them). I contrast this with my own societies, Australia and England, where fear is omnipresent; it is, in fact, a way of life, and Britain, with its five million plus CCTV cameras is a deserved object of ridicule (see *The Simpsons* episode where Britain's example of extreme public surveillance is tried in 'Springfield' and leads to a mass revolt against the proto-fascist Big Brother society).

Fear of North Korea is deeply entrenched in certain societies, not least in Japan. A close friend in Osaka described the situation to me in mid-2011; 'we are told every day by our media that North Korea is planning to attack us with every bomb at its disposal'. I mentioned this to my teaching colleagues in Pyongyang and they could not believe anyone would be so insane (their word) as to believe this; only a madman, they told me, would even think of such a possibility, and, of course, they are perfectly correct. On a brighter note, a few days after I left Pyongyang in December 2011, I was in Osaka and I saw something I had never seen before. The local TV news had a report from the DPRK. It was a curiosity; it asked the question, 'what has happened to....?' and it mentioned a name which I do not now recall. It belonged to a North Korean newsreader and TV presenter, a woman regarded, in Japan at least, as the media face of North Korea over many years. In recent weeks, however, she had disappeared from the screen. What struck me about this lengthy and detailed Japanese press story was that it was so lacking in any kind of hostility or suspicion. Rather, it seemed to be admiring of this woman's longevity, her force of character even, and to be showing real concern for her health. It was a rare example in Japan, or elsewhere, of viewing North Korea as a place of people 'just like us'.

By mid-December I was back at the family home in England. Within a day or so, the leader of North Korea died of a heart attack in his late sixties. I had the misfortune to catch the ITN News report on TV; it used the footage from Pyongyang but the journalist's voiceover (he was, of course, not in Pyongyang and probably had never been there) raised doubt about the genuineness of the tears of those shown weeping, raised fears about the security of the world now that a youth was in charge of a nuclear power (a nuclear test apparently makes one a nuclear power), and dismissed the deceased Kim Jong'il as 'an odious tyrant'.

The last press photo I saw of Kim Jong'il in December 2011 was of him inspecting the recently-opened Kaesong Youth Park in central Pyongyang. It is a fun park, filled with the kind of stomach-turning, spine-twisting rides that children adore, plus electric bumper-cars and other such diversions. It opens in the evenings during the week and, according to one of the schoolgirls I taught, stays open until 1am (for those hardy enough to brave temperatures of minus nine degrees or for those working nightshifts, I cannot say). The park has been an enormous success. It is so popular that in an ongoing exhibition of paintings at the Mansudae Art Studio, among all the studies of tigers, workers, and mountain landscapes, one of the major paintings is of a group of children on the most thrilling of these rides. In passing, another of the paintings in the exhibition is of the 'modern girl' of Pyongyang, elegantly and colourfully dressed, walking down a Pyongyang avenue, and fixated absolutely on the mobile 'phone in her hand.

One of the fixed ideas about Kim Jong'il is that he was reclusive, presumably terrified to go out from the safety of his tyranny, certainly terrified to leave the safety of the North. Shortly before his death, however, he had travelled quietly to the Russian Far East and had a series of meetings with the Russian president, Medvedev. The aim was to improve Korea's access to gas and other energy supplies, and, more generally, to drum up business. The North would love to see trade and investment come in from the outside; the mobile 'phone network was apparently set up with Egyptian investment, one of the most popular beers in Korea is now imported from Argentina, and there are cars on the roads of Pyongyang from every country (including the U.S.). Indeed, anyone wishing to do business with the DPRK can use the services of a gentlemanly Scots lawyer who has been based in Pyongyang for about seven years; he has a website, and an office at the Pyongyang Hotel. North Korea is not a hermit state or a paranoid peninsula. It has long-standing mutually beneficial ties with two of the most important countries on earth; Russia which literally is the powerhouse (it has all the energy) in Europe, and China which historically has been the dominant power in Asia and is now simply retaking that position. Critics may say that North Korea is an economic burden to China, and perhaps also to Russia, but the truth is that it provides a cast-iron guarantee of security to both of those states in a strategically vital part of Northeast Asia. They will not allow such a long-standing and indomitable ally to fall.

But I am remiss. We must try to remember that North Korea is the 'most repressive society on earth' and that Kim Jong'il was 'an odious tyrant'. To test these ideas, we may venture into the classrooms of Pyongyang. First point: I was frequently left entirely alone with the children, these innocent and impressionable fourteen year olds, both male and female. When a fellow teacher was in the classroom, it was for two reasons; either he or she was the teacher of this particular class and wanted to see what they were learning, or it was another teacher who would ask me if he or she could sit in solely out of a desire to learn something for themselves (the teachers were particularly fascinated by a book of tongue-twisters that I took for them and were regularly to be seen practicing 'she sells sea shells... '; they just enjoyed the pleasure of language as a game). No-one at any point in any of my hundreds of hours in charge of schoolchildren in Pyongyang has ever said to me, you cannot, or should not, say that (whatever it may be): no-one has ever said, you should not have said that (whatever it may have been). On an earlier occasion, I took a copy of The Simpsons comic book to show the students what a comic in other countries might look like. One of the teachers said, 'Oh, that's the one where the mother has a strange hairstyle!' They already knew about it. Another teacher told me that he has access to Google; he is not in any special position of authority, he is just a teacher. But we must remember that this is 'the most repressive society on earth' and that Kim Jong'il is 'an odious tyrant'.

What of the children's view of Kim, then? His photo is hung in classrooms but, as far as I can recall, not in every classroom. If it appears, it is always beside the photo of his father, Kim Ilsung, and they both look just like senior schoolboys (young, short-haired, without glasses, in high-collared uniform, looking for once, stern and serious, not relaxed or happy). The most common place to see images of Kim Jong'il in Pyongyang is in the feel-good roadside hoardings (again, almost always with Kim Ilsung beside him), all bright colours, smiles, optimistic outlook. A British newspaper once reported that North Korean television ONLY shows pictures of Kim Jong'il and of the military. Really? We are back to that science-fiction alternative universe. From what I have observed, the most common image on North Korean TV is of someone, young or old, singing or playing music: no sign of Kim Jong'il, and not much of the military (except when it is providing the singers). In terms of images, we must also ponder the curiosity of a 'tyrant' who allows the most common public image – the lapel badge – to be dominated by his father's image rather than his own (I have never seen anyone wearing a lapel badge with Kim Jong'il's photo, only that of Kim Ilsung).

The book *North Korea:The Paranoid Peninsula* argues that every aspect of schooling is related back to the Kim dynasty. Of course, if one were a tyrant, this is probably what one would do. But then, here lies a mystery (the schoolboys I talked to love mysteries, as well as explorers, inventors, and strange phenomena of all types and guises, so let us delve into this one). It is rooted in the fact that in the English-language textbook used in every school across North Korea for fourteen year-olds, there is barely a single mention of Kim Jong'il or even of Kim Ilsung. Instead, there are, for example, lessons on 'Being Creative', the science of 'What happens to us when we sleep?', and ones specifically on the history of Ireland, South Africa, and the Maoris of New Zealand. In the latter, the schoolchildren are given various terms from the Maori languages to learn. They are also told about the heroic resistance of the

Maoris to European colonisation and how they have worked to maintain their unique cultural identity. No mention of Kim Jong'il (not even the possibility that the Maoris may have gained their fortitude by studying his works). The mystery continues.

One of the finest speeches in the English language comes, unsurprisingly perhaps, from Shakespeare. It is not the soliloquy by Hamlet nor is it Macbeth's tortured 'is this a dagger I see before me?' It is, instead, that remarkable speech given by Mark Antony in *Julius Caesar*, beginning with 'Friends, Romans, countryman...' but at the heart of which is the recurring, and increasingly accusatory and damning, refrain 'But Brutus says it is so and Brutus is an honourable man.' The schoolchildren I taught have heard about various famous names from other countries, such as Gandhi, Nelson Mandela, and the great explorers like Magellan and James Cook (they have also heard of another Englishman, Chaplin, through a documentary shown recently on North Korean TV but that is just by-the-by). I did not ask them if they have ever heard of Shakespeare but on my next visit perhaps we should practice Antony's speech. They already understand irony. I know because we spent several class hours listening to some very witty jokes, including ones using irony, which they translated from North Korean joke books (and no teacher or official ever said to me, you cannot do this!).

There are at least two major flaws in the dealing of countries like the US, Britain and Australia with North Korea. One is that they show no respect. Without respect, there can be no progress in talks and no security in co-existence. The Korean schoolchildren whom I taught in 2011 were, and are, enormously proud of their society; they see themselves as engaged in a great endeavour, still incomplete, but with constant steps towards improvement (the massive construction projects of 2011 plus the spread of mobile 'phones and computer technology are just some examples of this progress). Yet, no-one, pupil or teacher, ever made a derogatory or disrespectful comment to me about any other society (only about the leaders of some countries). At the heart of respect for others is the ability to reflect on oneself. If we were to see ourselves from the Korean perspective, what would stand out among the good and the bad? The fragmentation of our communities is obvious. The corruption of our leaders is obvious; it is not just Bush, Blair and Howard conspiring to wage aggressive war against Iraq, or the fact that Blair, instead of being on trial, is still attempting to provoke war with Iran (let us all ignore the losses in Iran during its eight-year war against the Western-backed Iraq and kill more Iranian men and women). It is not just Berlusconi with his criminal indictments longer than most inhabitants of our overcrowded and hopeless prisons. We have leaders who tell us that they are taking 'tough decisions' when what they are actually doing, because they have no solution, is further destroying our social capital, our primary asset in facing future challenges far greater than the national debt which hypnotises them presently. Looking at all this, perhaps North Korean citizens would see themselves as fortunate and feel sympathy for us; after all, they apparently retain a sense of community and they have leaders who still talk of progress despite privation, not doctors addressing a terminally ill patient with yet more harsh measures and acts of 'bleeding' (see the philosopher Jacques Rancière on 'doctors and democracy'). But if the North Koreans were to look at our culture, our TV and film, what then would they see, and would they still pity us? I suspect they would be appalled at our addiction to horror – look at the evening's TV and the number of programmes dealing with murder, or that sub-genre of the horror movie in recent years, 'torture porn'. Look at the fear of citizen towards citizen; the locked doors of the aged and the caging of our children against unseen predators at every corner (read Frank Furedi's works for an overview of our 'culture of fear'). Are we not in the same situation that the great philosopher-critic Walter Benjamin observed in 1930s Europe, where so many members of our society are so alienated from each other and the society itself is so fragmented and failed that we sub-consciously hope for its annihilation? The society Benjamin was describing was Nazi Germany and that should give us pause for thought about how our adoration of death, misery and cruelty as entertainment, as well as our complacency in the face of our own political hypocrisy and corruption, makes us seem in the eyes of others.

The second flaw in our dealing with North Korea is the refusal to think of that country's leader as anything but 'an odious tyrant'. If one allows that the Kim family is not tyrannical, and that the people of North Korea willingly maintain the existing system because it offers them security from enemies with more guns and money (and aggressive intent) than they, then the entire, nakedly racist attitude towards North Korea begins to crumble; and then what would James Bond do for his next Fu Manchu-style Oriental villain? What would we all do for a pantomime 'Oriental', merciless, inhumane, and so utterly evil that we could all comfortably, and comfortingly, hate him and wish him 'taken out'. If the Kim family is not populated with tyrants and madmen, then there must be another reason (in fact, a very cogent and, even for us, understandable reason) for the North Korean determination to possess nuclear weapons: it might even have something to do with our own overt hatred and contempt, that hatred and contempt which used to be directed at China a century ago, was then transferred to Japan in the 1900s, went back to China in the 1950s, and now shines bright on Korea. But, with a leader in Pyongyang who is neither a tyrant nor a madman, the entire military logic of sustaining immense forces in readiness for an outbreak of war (which has never come since 1950 and, at least since the 1970s, was never even likely to come) begins to stumble. With a leader in Pyongyang who is neither a tyrant nor a madman, the entire political logic of endless sanctions begins to crumble (will they be applied to Saudi Arabia when it develops its own nuclear weapons in response to those of Iran?). Instead, with a leader who is neither a tyrant nor a madman, the possibility of giving and receiving respect, of exchanging ideas, of coming to an accommodation, and of reducing hostility and hatred, which thereby defuses the fear behind nuclear weapons, begins actually to be plausible. But, of course, I am forgetting once more. North Korea is the 'most repressive state on earth' and the leader of North Korea is, was, will be, an 'odious tyrant'. Our leaders and our media consistently tell us this, and they are honourable men.

Last Tour of Duty

It is May 2012 and, again, I am in Beijing. Kōichi and I are in one of the airport coffee shops; he is bringing me up to date on news from the North. The major talking point is about a Chinese fishing boat captain's complaint. He accuses the North Koreans of trying to extort money from him (I assume they have impounded his boat). The sums involved are not large, and it seems the captain does not challenge the Korean claim that he was fishing in their waters. This kind of thing has happened before – and as fish stocks decline, will certainly happen with greater frequency and violence – but no-one in China has previously gone to the public for sympathy. I have often observed that there is little human warmth in relations between China and Korea. Chinese popular criticism of Korea in this dispute only affirms my view.

We also talk briefly about the death of Kim Jong'il. I ask Kōichi if he noticed the vehicle used as a hearse to carry Kim's body. It was an old Lincoln Continental. I wonder at the choice of a car identified with 1960s American presidents. Kim was said to have been a fan of The Beach Boys, among other groups, and a great admirer of the basketball player Michael

Jordan. Perhaps the choice of hearse was a further reflection of his American tastes. How the car first came to be in the North, however, would surely make for an interesting story.

On this working visit, the deal is that I will be attached exclusively to the Middle School in the city centre. This is to compensate the School for my enforced exile, due to its untimely renovations, on my previous stay. I will keep in touch with my former pupils at the College only on afternoons in my second week when I will cross the city and join them for informal classes and, I have no doubt, an occasional game of football.

As a guest of the Middle School, it is the dapper Teacher Ham who is to be my regular companion. He is as boyish-looking as ever. He and I are ensconced in a hotel new to me. This is Ansan Lodge, a pretty one-storey building set beside its own large pond and in trees beyond which is the quiet-flowing River Potong. Early in the morning and at weekends I see kayaks drifting seamlessly down the river. Teacher Ham takes a stroll around the pond or beside the river every morning, relishing the freshness and quiet of a spring dawn.

At the School, I am introduced to my four new classes. As usual, there are about 25 boys in each. Quickly, I learn that some of these boys are among the most gifted of all the several hundred I have taught in Pyongyang to date. Teaching, thus, becomes very easy. When I ask a question, there are always several replies at least; no longer do I have to force a response by counting down, '5,4,3,2,1…' and threatening to leave as I had to do with some of my earliest classes. In one of these new groups, there is a unique student; though only fourteen, he delights in taking a contrary position to everyone else, including me (were I, for example, to say it is morning, he would undoubtedly have said, 'ah yes, but elsewhere in the world it is night'). And I do mean that he delights in this; for him, language and discussion is a game to be relished. For every question I put to his class, he is ready with a long and complex answer, or even two. It reaches the point where I have to assign him a time quota; if I didn't do this, he would monopolise the lion's share of every lesson. Later, in an informal conversation class of five boys, I give him and the others all the time they wish (two hours and we were still talking).

In another of the classes, there are two boys who, again only 14-15, are about 6' tall. One of them is a very genial fellow, always smiling and relaxed; in class, I nickname him Mr. Periscope, for no particular reason but the name seems to work and stays in place. The other boy is more intense and more heavily involved in the questions and answers. He also stands out as the most naturally gifted of the Frisbee players in the school. I always take a handful of Frisbees for after-class games and as parting gifts. Some boys take time to work out the aerodynamics of the disc – it appears they have never seen them before – and the school principal, no matter how many times I show him, always makes a complete hash of it, flicking it over even before it leaves his hand so that it just tumbles miserably to the ground. The tall student, however, standing well above the principal, just launches the thing into a perfect arc with effortless grace. I think of him as a Frisbee-slinging Billy the Kid.

The Frisbees were very popular being such a light and simple game. They did, however, lead to some unexpected complications. One afternoon, following our usual small-group conversation class, I took the boys into the courtyard and we started throwing the Frisbee. As often happened, some of the youngest boys and girls clustered nearby – though not too near;

these smaller children were anxious in my presence and there was often a worried 'ooohh' if I loomed above them. I determined to overcome this and sent a second Frisbee into the crowd. It landed near a small girl of about eleven. She reached down to pick it up and then froze, uncertain what to do next. I went up to her – 'ooohhs' from some of the others – and told her in Korean that it was a gift. She just looked innocently at me so I told her again but, quite to my surprise, her impish girlfriend beside her began to repeat my every word in a laughing sing-song voice. Here I was being mocked by an infant! No sign of fear, but also no sign of respect. I told this unwelcome sprite to go away but she just repeated my words again and stood her ground, laughing. The upshot of all of this is that I left the first girl with the Frisbee in her hand but, for whatever reason, she could not believe it was really a gift and, the next morning, she and her friend ceremoniously returned it to the boys in my class. I had to ask them in turn to find the girl and restore it to her.

A similarly complicated situation arose with a group of the younger boys, also about eleven years old. As I was waiting for my car at the end of the day, about four of them passed me on the school entrance steps and, as was usual, bowed. One of them, however, also said hello and, naturally, I replied. This brought about some giggling as they carried on their way. Then, in silent agreement, they just halted a short distance from Teacher Ham and I, and waited. I saw another chance for a little ice-breaking and asked Teacher Ham for one of the last Frisbees in our bag. He took it out and motioned to the pupils to get ready. They must have seen us playing before as they quickly got the hang of it. We threw back and forth for about five minutes and then my car drew up. I called the boys to me and told them I had to leave. I said, however, that I would leave the Frisbee in their collective care and that they should return it to me two days hence at this same time. That was the signal for the first of the complications: as Teacher Ham and I walked away, a great free-for-all scuffle broke out, small bodies rolling on the concrete, to decide who would be master of the object. It seems I had overestimated the absence of the possessive instinct in a socialist state. Teacher Ham intervened as referee and nominated one of the boys; it was his job to look after the Frisbee and see to its return.

The next day, Teacher Ham and I were walking up the central stairway to the third floor. As we talked, various pupils passed and bowed. There were generally two forms of bow; a shallow bow on the run, or a more elaborate stop and bow. Among the pupils this morning at one of the turns in the stairwell, a couple of small boys stopped, bowed deeply, and, unusually, came up smiling. I was too lost in whatever I was saying to take too much notice and merely nodded in return. Teacher Ham stopped and said, "Don't you recognise them? They are the boys you spoke to yesterday." The pair had already headed off down the stairs, no doubt disappointed at my lack of response. Thanks to Teacher Ham's prompting, I still had time to call after them, "see you tomorrow boys!" They turned and rewarded me with another smile.

The following afternoon, I was in the last stage of a game of cricket with one of my class at the time I'd agreed to meet the young ones. I asked one of my class to go round to the entrance and let them know I would be a few minutes late. He soon returned and reported no sign of anyone there. I was surprised because, despite their youth, the faces and the words of these children had convinced me they could be trusted. There was nothing I could do so I let the matter drop and finished off the game in hand. As we packed up, I noticed that the last of the Frisbees had gone missing. I had let some of the milling pupils play with this while the rest of were cricketing but I wanted to keep it close as a final day present for the natural thrower I dubbed Billy the Kid. Its disappearance was annoying but none of my class had a clue as to its fate. Irritated, I set off to find my car. As we entered the forecourt, the four young boys came round the corner, all relieved smiles and explaining that they had come at our agreed time and repeatedly since then. My original intention had been to give them the Frisbee in their care as a parting gift but now, with the loss of the other one, I was in two minds. But this lasted only a moment: they had been friendly, lively, respectful and responsible. It was a pleasure to see their faces light up as I informed them – and Teacher Ham reiterated the point to avoid misunderstanding – that the Frisbee was now theirs as a group, with the proviso that they work out a system for sharing it.

The story, however, had yet a final twist. On my last day, I walked into one of the classrooms. On the desk was a Frisbee. I asked where it had come from. A boy in the second row replied that he and others had spotted it in the hands of a group of younger males and confiscated it as 'the missing Frisbee'. This was despite the children's entreaties that it had been a gift from the English teacher. I asked my class, on their honour, to return this Frisbee to its new and rightful owners. Then, later that day, I was told that other, anonymous pupils had returned the last Frisbee and that, as I had instructed, it had been given to 'Billy'. I did wonder to myself whether, on my next visit, I should bring even more Frisbees, or was that just asking for ever greater trouble!

Being May, it is also time for the School's Sports Day. The event takes place in the parkland beside the Potong River, only a short walk across from my hotel. As a guest of the School, I sit at the principal's table and am occasionally tasked with handing out a prize. It seems that most, if not all, of the pupils are involved in some event, and so are many of the teachers. The large crowd of spectators is composed mainly of relatives enjoying a picnic. As for the sports, they are easily recognisable; a mix of genuine athletic challenge and a willingness to make oneself look silly. In one game, team members have to hurl themselves onto a balloon and burst it without using their hands. A favourite technique here is to drop from above and use one's chest, though this works less well with the older, more shapely girls. Next, the contestant has to roll a ball several metres and knock over a skittle; a team member rolls back the ball if it misses. Having accomplished all this, the last task is to bob for an apple in a bucket of coloured powder. Everyone, of course, comes running back to the line, face ablaze with dusty streaks of colour.

In between events, two ensembles of girls dance to entertain the crowd. Older ones dressed in the brilliantly-coloured long skirts and shining silk blouses of the traditional Korean costume perform elegant classical moves. Smaller girls with skinny limbs are in leotards and Disney-style animal masks; half are chubby-cheeked piglets and half are moon-faced kittens. They offer a comic dance of chase and escape, full of head-rocking and little gloved fists shaking in mock fright or delight. Even the most hardened and world weary cynic, and after thirty years of visiting Japan, the kingdom of atrocious cute, that includes me, would have to concede that they are genuinely cute and charming.

There is, of course, a reminder that Sports Days are not solely about fun, especially in a garrison state. Some of the older males and females are sent on a long-distance run complete with heavy backpacks; they return later drenched in sweat. Others compete in a race of stretcher-bearers. The bearers are all girls and those borne, complete with arms in slings, are all male. As Teacher Ham explains, in war, men fight and women nurse. Despite this grim backdrop, there is general hilarity from the crowd and other pupils whenever the bearers stumble and the suffering 'hero' goes flying.

Since my last visit, of course, there has been a change of leadership. The youthful Kim Jong'un is now the head of the country and Kōichi has asked me to observe people's reactions to him. One of the senior teachers makes an interesting distinction for me; the deceased father was often stiff in the company of others, the newly-elevated son is often filmed or photographed in an intimate huddle with everyone from generals to workers. There is a greater sense of warmth and, naturally, of vitality with the young man. Some of the stories I hear to illustrate his virtues include the report that he held back the announcement of his father's death for some hours so that the people might still enjoy what was left of their weekend. It is offered as an example of caring for others even in the midst of personal grief. Such stories, and the value placed on them, reinforce the view that the Kim dynasty is presented domestically, and perceived very much, as a Confucian leadership in which benevolence and a sense of the leader as father of the people is central.

On TV, I see a recurring montage of Kim Jong'un. First, he is shown as a kind of Mongol warrior, dressed in simple jacket and trousers but astride a magnificent horse in the hills; in this, he looks like a big man, exuding strength and energy. Then he is shown laughing and mixing easily with crowds of soldiers or workers, a man of the people (in contrast with his austere father). Cut in between these shots, however, is what I take to be the key point of it all; it is footage of the young Kim Ilsung and the emphasis is firmly on the close resemblance in face and hairstyle of the two men. The implicit message appears to be: now we return to greatness.

The death of Kim Jong'il and the ascent of Kim Jong'un led to a violence of feeling unprecedented in my experience. It was directed at the conservative South Korean president, Lee Myungbak. Normally, not much is said in Pyongyang about 'the other Korea', except that there is only one Korean people, and that the government in the South betrays the Korean people through its alliance with the U.S. Now, I see on TV and in the press, and I hear even from normally gentle people, bitter hatred of Lee. In the media, he is shown repeatedly as a rodent – human face on rat body - being butchered or garrotted (Lee's nickname in South Korea is 'Rat' so the North Korean media has a ready-made image for this hate). At issue once again is the question of morality and of benevolence versus malevolence. Lee, I am told by some of the teachers, banned any South Korean from attending the funeral of Kim Jong'il; to people in the North, this is seen as an inhuman level of disrespect. Further, Lee is said to have boasted that the South Korean military, perhaps using a drone or guided missile, could kill Kim Jong'un anytime, anywhere. For people in Pyongyang, to speak so glibly of murdering a young man only just come to power is seen as the act of a gangster or hoodlum.

A counterpoint to the South Korean president's disrespect is a TV program I see one evening. It is, to me at least, a rare program about Kim Ilsung. It is composed entirely of the same scene, played and replayed over the years; foreign dignitaries, be they presidents (or ex-presidents in the case of Jimmy Carter), prime ministers, or diplomats, all being greeted in Pyongyang by Kim Ilsung. For most of these scenes, Kim is dressed in his usual suit and tie, and the only indications of the passage of time are the greying of his hair and the shift of film stock from b/w to colour. Many of the dignitaries bring gifts, including awards of medals and sashes; the most flamboyant of these come from the postcolonial African republics, either because of their natural love of colour or as an act of defiance for their unenviable place in the new world order. In its endless repetition of the same scene, however, (even the number of steps forward Kim takes towards his guest seems unvarying), the program appears to hammer home its message: we are not isolated and many nations across the world treat us with respect.

On this trip, I observe something else I had never witnessed before, even when I visited other cities in 2006. One lunchtime, I am walking with Teacher Ham in the large park opposite the School. Filled with fountains, statues, and quiet benches, it is a favourite place for wedding photos, and there is always a line of cars and mini-buses disgorging newly-married brides in their bright outfits along with their husbands, relatives and friends. To avoid these busy groups, we go further into the park and take a secluded bench. A short distance away there is a female university student in her long, dark blue skirt reading a book. As we sit in the sun, grateful that so far, at least, the great sandstorms from China have not blanketed the sky this spring, we see a girl approach the student. She is about 11 or 12, long hair in a pony-tail, and dressed in dark shirt and trousers. She stands stiffly before the student and bows deeply. Then, still at attention, she waits in silence. Within a second or two, the student reaches into her bag and, without a word, hands something to the girl. The girl bows deeply again and walks away. I turn to Teacher Ham and ask him, 'Was that little girl begging?' He nods. 'Yes, we too have unfortunate people. Perhaps her parents are ill or have done something wrong?' He looks genuinely troubled for the girl. As we walk back to the school, we can still see her, striding up the hill. Teacher Ham leaves me and goes quickly up to her. As he calls out, I can see her stand and turn, completely without fear. I see Teacher Ham reach into his wallet; the girl stands stiffly as before, bows, and walks away, all in silence. When Teacher Ham rejoins me, I ask him, 'How much did you give her?' It is the wrong question. It is, in fact, a thoughtless question. He just opens his wallet to show me; it is empty. Tomorrow, his relative is to marry and I know he is to provide all the drinks for the wedding guests. I ask him what will he do. He replies that he will just sign for the bottles – the shopkeeper knows him – and will then pay when he gets his wages. I do not want to embarrass him but, later, I hand him some euros; my gift, I explain, to him and his family on their day of celebration. Tomorrow, he and the new couple will be back in this park for photos. To myself, I wonder if the girl will also be back.

As I am posted to the Middle School on this trip, I only visit the College occasionally, and really just to say a brief hello to the five classes of boys and one of girls I had taught the previous year. En route to one of these classes, Teacher Kim stopped me on the steps of the west building and said, 'There is one of your students – see, he is wearing the watch you gave him." It was Tiger (I no longer attach the ugly word 'killer', even in jest). He was sweeping the entrance. He was taller and slimmer than when I had last seen him; his voice was also deeper but still had that richness to it that I remembered so well. I asked how he was, and he replied that he was fine, working hard at his new subjects, and enjoying the challenge of being tested at a higher level. I also asked him if the watch was still keeping good time; he confirmed that it was. 'Remarkable," I said, 'for a cheap watch given as a joke prize.' I had got it on Ebay and awarded it for the best joke in Tiger's class. 'Yes,' he replied, 'you told me it only cost one cent but, for me, it is valuable because it was you gave it to me.' I had to smile again at this young man: only in his mid-teens, he was so easily able to express a mature and sophisticated thought, even in a foreign language, and to do it with eloquence. Unlike virtually every one of the other boys, Tiger never showed any interest in football and so he did not join us in the matches which usually followed these visits. Indeed, that brief meeting on the steps was to be our last.

Another person I was to see again all too briefly was the Russian-language guide at Mangyongdae. Manager Kim frequently joked that my 'Russian' ladyfriend was waiting for my return and, one Sunday, he arranged for us to go back with a small group of boys from the School. Being May, the site was filled with coachloads of visitors. There were hundreds of women, many in bright, flowing dresses like tropical birds – light pinks, sky blues, and canary yellows – and hundreds of men, all dressed like ravens in a graveyard in suits of black, charcoal and grey. I had commented once to Teacher Kim that North Korean women must be very disappointed in their men; their appearance (with a few exceptions such as Teacher Ham and Manager Kim who often favoured light browns) was painfully dull. He just smiled, as he always did, and answered, as he always did, 'Probably.'

Once the guide arrived, she apologised for the press of people and led us quickly into the queue circling the Kim family's tiny compound. There, she told me that, as I had heard the story so many times before, she would not give me the usual narrative. Instead, and here the mischievous glint in her eye should have warned me, she would ask me to explain about the various objects on display. This put me on the spot and I could see the boys watching on in anticipation. I'm afraid, however, I stumbled and fumbled even at the first question; clearly I was not an apt pupil. The gods, however, took pity that day on a poor atheist and our guide was suddenly whisked away by the arrival of a Russian TV crew.

A further site I was to revisit was the Chongnyon Hotel coffee shop. Since the winter, it had been completely renovated; new walls of wood panelling for warmth and internal screens for privacy. Ms. Pak and the other waitresses also had a smart, new uniform. The place was busy with customers, all youngish men preoccupied with mobile 'phones. Manager Kim had his usual chat with the waitresses and Teacher Kim his usual glass of beer followed by a cigarette. I, however, felt that something had been lost in the change and no longer wished to linger.

With Manager Kim on these final evenings in the tiny bar of the Ansan Lodge, most of the talk (when we could distract his attention from the mature but charming waitress) was about the future. I was already committed to returning in December, then again the following April for a longer time, during which I would teach not only at my two existing schools but also at one in another city (Nampo on the west coast was suggested). In addition, I had offered to buy tickets for him and two teachers, one from each of the present schools, to visit and establish links with educational institutions in New Zealand. We discussed who would best serve the interests of the schools and, by extension, the country if this visit took place. My own thought was that a combination of Teacher Ham and either Mrs. Song or Mrs. Kwak would work very well; I was imagining the reaction of New Zealand schoolchildren on being introduced to teachers from North Korea and I knew that any of these three would instantly leave an impression of gentleness. That, after all, had been my abiding impression over the two years while I had been working in Pyongyang and was, I believed, the message needed to counter the entrenched imagery in the West of repression, fear or belligerence. Manager Kim just listened and smiled, probably dreaming of new possibilities for his schools, maybe a chance to cultivate foreign investment, of enjoying fine wine and food, and, no doubt, of meeting some beautiful Maori ladies

Closing at an End

Three days after leaving Pyongyang, I had something of a Kafkaesque moment. Instead of waking up as a giant insect, however, I woke to find myself suddenly and inexplicably paralysed in all four limbs. For eight months I remained in hospital, unable either to stand, walk, or, for much of that time, even to use my fingers to press the nurse's call-bell. Never before had the words of Seneca, which I had applied frequently to the people in Pyongyang, seemed so personally relevant. When, finally, I left the hospital, I remained confined to a wheelchair and unable to use the hands for much of anything. This was not quite what I had planned for 2013. It meant, of course, that I was unable to fulfil my promise to the teachers and pupils of the two schools to return. Fortunately, I was still able through my wife to buy tickets for two teachers and one of my contacts to make the planned visit to New Zealand. In the end, the party included Teacher Kim representing the College and another male teacher called Kim representing the School. Manager Kim, who was looking forward to the trip, was transferred to another post before the party left Pyongyang and so, much to his regret no doubt, he did not travel. This redeployment also means that, if I ever recover and make it back to Pyongyang, he will not be there at the airport to greet me nor at the hotel to tell me, 'Such beautiful ladies!' I suspect, however, I need only listen carefully enough at restaurants and cafés across the city and, somewhere, I will hear his great, booming laugh. It is something which I look forward to, as indeed I do to catching up with all of the good people I have met in that city. There, I have started a job; as long as it remains unfinished, then so am I. This is not entirely altruism or even a sense of duty. After all, it is in the classrooms of Pyongyang that I, as a teacher, have the greatest fun.

www.ingramcontent.com/pod-product-compliance
Lightning Source LLC
Chambersburg PA
CBHW080253290526
45790CB00005B/1798